FOOTPATHS OF BRITAIN

SOUTH-WEST

p

This is a Parragon Book
First published in 2003

Parragon
Queen Street House
4 Queen Street
Bath BA1 1HE
United Kingdom

Created and produced by
The Bridgewater Book Company Ltd,
Lewes, East Sussex

ISBN: 1-40540-507-4

Printed in China

www.walkingworld.com

Visit the Walkingworld website at
www.walkingworld.com

All the walks in this book are available in more
detailed form on the Walkingworld website.
The route instructions have photographs at key
decision points to help you to navigate, and
each walk comes with an Ordnance Survey®
map. Simply print them out on A4 paper
and you are ready to go! A modest annual
subscription gives you access to over 1,400
walks, all in this easy-to-follow format. If you
wish, you can purchase individual walks for a
small fee.

Next to every walk in this book you will see
a Walk ID. You can enter this ID number on
Walkingworld's 'Find a Walk' page and you will
be taken straight to the details of that walk.

CONTENTS

Introduction

Britain is a fabulous place to walk. We are blessed with a varied and beautiful landscape, a dense network of public footpaths and places of historical interest at every corner. Add to all this the many thousands of well-placed pubs, tea shops and visitor attractions, and it's easy to see why walking is a treasured pastime for millions of people.

Walking is the perfect way to keep fit and healthy. It is good for your heart, muscles and body generally, without making the extreme demands of many sports. For most walkers, however, the health benefits are secondary. We walk for the sheer pleasure of it – being able to breathe in the fresh air, enjoy the company of our friends and 'get away from it all'.

Equipment

If you take up walking as a hobby, it is quite possible to spend a fortune on specialist outdoor kit. But you really don't need to. Just invest in a few inexpensive basics and you'll be ready to enjoy any of the walks in this book.

For footwear, boots are definitely best as they provide you with ankle support and protection from the inevitable mud, nettles and puddles. A light-weight pair should be fine if you have no intention of venturing up big hills or over rugged terrain. If you are not sure what to get, go to a specialist shop and ask for advice. Above all, choose boots that fit well and are comfortable.

Take clothing to deal with any weather that you may encounter. Allow for the 'wind-chill' factor – if your clothes get wet you will feel this cooling effect even more. Carry a small rucksack with a spare top, a hat and waterproofs, just in case. The key is being able to put on and take off layers of clothing at will and so keep an even, comfortable temperature throughout the day.

It's a good idea to carry some food and drink. Walking is exercise and you need to replace the fluid you lose through perspiration. Take a bottle of soft drink or water, and sip it regularly rather than downing it in one go. The occasional chocolate bar, sandwich or biscuit can work wonders when energy levels are flagging.

Walking poles – the modern version of the walking stick – are worth considering. They help you to balance and allow your arms to take some of the strain when going uphill. They also lessen the impact on your knees on downhill slopes. Don't be fooled into thinking that poles are just for the older walker – they are popular with trekkers and mountaineers of all ages.

Finding your way

Most walkers use Ordnance Survey® maps, rightly considered to be among the most accurate, up-to-date and 'walker-friendly' in the world. The 1:50,000 scale Landranger series has long been a favourite of outdoor enthusiasts. Almost all areas of Britain are also covered by the more detailed 1:25,000 scale Explorer and Explorer OL series. These include features such as field boundaries, farm buildings and small streams.

Having a map and compass – and learning how to use them – is vital to being safe in the countryside. Compass and map skills come with practice – there is no substitute for taking them out and having a go. Buy a compass with a transparent base plate and rotating dial; you will find this type in any outdoor shop. Most come with simple instructions – if not, ask in the shop for a guide.

If this all sounds a bit serious, I urge you not to worry too much about getting lost. We have all done it – some of us more often than we care to admit! You are unlikely to come to much harm unless you are on a featureless hilltop or out in very poor weather. If you want to build up your confidence, start with shorter routes through farmland or along the coastline and allow yourself plenty of time.

key to maps

Telephone			Lighthouse
Start of walk			Camping
Viewpoint			Youth hostel
Pylon			Bridge
Triangulation point			Windmill
Radio mast			Highest point/summit
Church with Steeple		PH	Public house
Church without Steeple		PC	Public convenience
Chapel		1666	Place of historical interest
Power lines			Embankment/cutting
Golf course			Rocky area/ sharp drop
Picnic area			Building
Car park			Castle
Information			Tumulus
			Garden

There are plenty of walks in this book that are perfect for the beginner. You can make navigating even easier by downloading the routes in this book from Walkingworld's website: www.walkingworld.com. These detailed walk instructions feature a photograph at each major decision point, to help you confirm your position and see where to go next.

Another alternative is to join a local walking group

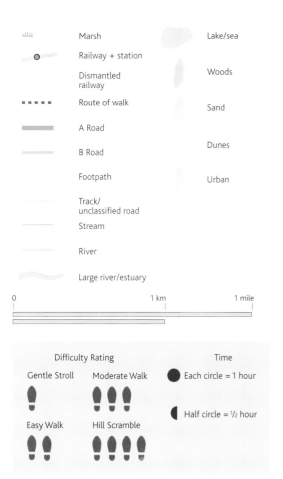

Marsh		Lake/sea	
Railway + station			
Dismantled railway		Woods	
Route of walk			
A Road		Sand	
B Road		Dunes	
Footpath		Urban	
Track/ unclassified road			
Stream			
River			
Large river/estuary			

0   1 km   1 mile

Difficulty Rating

Gentle Stroll   Moderate Walk

Easy Walk   Hill Scramble

Time

Each circle = 1 hour

Half circle = ½ hour

and learn from others. There are hundreds of such groups around the country, with members keen to share their experience and skills.

Enough words. Take the walks in this book as your inspiration. Grab your map and compass, and put on your boots. It's time to go out and walk!

Have fun.

DAVID STEWART *Walkingworld*

▲ Map: Explorer 164
▲ Distance: 11 km/6³/₄ miles
▲ Walk ID: 981 John Thorn

Difficulty rating

Time

▲ River, Sea, Castle, Birds, Great Views, Café, Food Shop, Good for Kids, Moor, Public Transport, Woodland, Ancient Monument

A484

49
48

Llanelli

47 46 45
44
Swansea 43
42
A4118

Port Talbot 41

Three Cliffs Bay from Penmaen

This is a circular walk from Penmaen through the woods and moorland to Three Cliffs Bay on the south coast of the Gower peninsula, a designated area of outstanding natural beauty.

1 Follow the track up the ridge. When you pass a stone marked 'Gower Way 12', bear right, following the track that skirts the woodland to your right. Just before the path divides, cross the stile on your right and follow the path into the woods as it opens out into a wider track. After a right-hand bend, go straight ahead at a crossroads (passing Gower Way stone 14).

2 At the crossroads at the bottom of a valley, turn right, following the track down. (Opposite on the left is Gower Way stone 15). The remnants of a prehistoric burial chamber will soon appear on your right.

3 Go through the gateway following a yellow arrow. Ignore the road on the left but turn left at the T-junction. On reaching the Gower Heritage Centre, continue straight ahead and cross the footbridge on the left. Continue along the road until you reach the main road.

4 Pass Shepherd's shop on your left and a house on your right. Turn right onto a path by a field gate. After 20 m, cross the footbridge and turn right, following a blue arrow. The path bears left over a hill. Ignore the left-hand path and continue ahead. The path opens out with a view of Pennard Castle. Continue down the left-hand side of the valley.

5 As you near the beach, continue ahead until you reach a ridge of pebbles, then turn right along the ridge and cross the stepping-stones. Do not take the path ahead marked by an arrow but turn left. Continue around the edge of the marsh with the hedge on your right. Go to the left of the sand dunes and emerge onto the beach.

6 Take the path to the top of the dunes. Follow the path that climbs up on the right-hand side of the holiday cottages. When you reach a stony track turn left, then turn right onto the road. Turn left at the T-junction. Cross the main road in front of the church and return to the start of the walk by following the narrow road on the right.

access information

Follow the A4118 along the Gower. Shortly after the Gower Inn at the Penmaen sign on the left-hand side, with the church in front of you, turn right on the narrow road. Follow this for about 200 yards, passing the care home on your left. When the road bears left, bear right onto the rough track and park on the grass.

Penmaen is accessible by bus, service 18 from Swansea.

The view from the cliffs at Three Cliffs Bay in Swansea makes the climb up the sand dunes worthwhile.

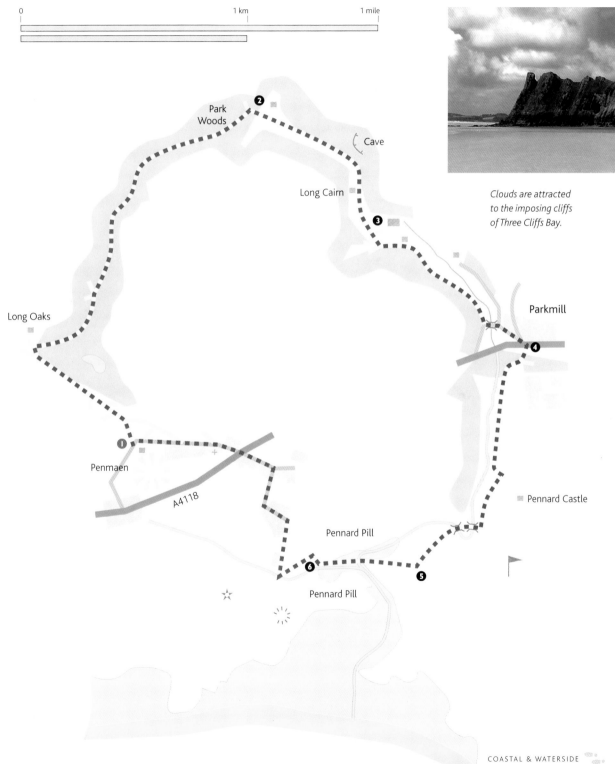

0   1 km   1 mile

Park Woods

2

Cave

Long Cairn

3

Clouds are attracted to the imposing cliffs of Three Cliffs Bay.

Parkmill

Long Oaks

4

1

Penmaen

Pennard Castle

A4118

Pennard Pill

6

Pennard Pill

5

▲ Map: Explorer 164
▲ Distance: 11 km/6¾ miles
▲ Walk ID: 966 John Thorn

Difficulty rating

Time

Hills or Fells, Sea, Pub, Toilets, National Trust, Birds, Flowers, Great Views, Café, Gift Shop, Public Transport, Ancient Monument

Burry Holms from Rhossili

This walk demonstrates much of the natural beauty of the Gower. From Rhossili, climb the Beacon, descend to Llangennith, cross the dunes to the beach, explore Burry Holms and return along the beach.

❶ From the car park entrance, walk to the left of a house with a white garage door, then turn left and follow the path around the church. Turn left, following the lane slightly downhill. Go through the gate marked 'Rhossili Down' and bear slightly right up the hill. After about 250 m the track levels out a bit. Bear slightly right then left to reach the trig point.

❷ Continue along the grassy track in the general direction of Llangennith, bearing left along the ridge. Where the path divides, bear left, aiming for the hilltop ahead with a rocky crag. From the top, follow the grassy track ahead with the steep hill down on your left. Ignore the path on the left.

❸ At a junction with a smaller path, turn right, heading in the direction of the large grey barn on the far hill. After 100 m, cross another path and bear left across the valley. Follow the path, making for the right-hand side of the small clump of trees to join a rough lane. Go through a gate, cross a stream and follow the road ahead into Llangennith.

❹ Turn left on the road following the sign marked 'Beach'. At the junction go ahead, following the road towards Broughton.

❺ At the entrance to the caravan park, cross the cattle grid and take the track on the left. After 150 m cross a stile. Just over the brow of the hill bear right. Cross another stile then fork right on the less well-defined path. Cross a fence at a stile and continue across the dunes. Turn right on the beach.

❻ Burry Holms Island can be reached at low tide. Having explored the island, retrace your steps to the beach and continue along the beach towards Rhossili. Just before the end of the beach, climb the steps to the left. After 100 m, turn right through a gate and continue uphill. Pass between the buildings to return to the car park.

access information

The walk starts from the car park at Rhossili, at the end of the B4247 west of the A4118. Buses 18, 18A, 18C, 18D run to Rhossili from Swansea; call First Cymru for info on 0870 6082608.

At high tide Burry Holms is inaccessible, although exploration of the island is possible when the sea retreats at low tide.

further information

• Do not follow this walk in poor visibility. Apart from missing the best views, some navigation depends on sighting far-away points.
• As you climb towards the trig point (point 2), you may see Lundy Island. Left of this is Clovelly, Ilfracombe and Exmoor as far as Minehead. To the right of Lundy are Pembroke and Tenby.
• Burry Holms has an Iron Age fort and various other relics.

This walk takes in a variety of interesting archaeological features including an Iron Age fort, as well as beautiful countryside.

6 Burry Holms

Llangennith Burrows

Dunes

Dunes

Dunes

5

P

PH

Llangennith

4

3

Rhossili Down

The Beacon

2

PH

Rhossili

1

P

0   1 km   1 mile

▲ Map: Explorer 164
▲ Distance: 8 km/5 miles
▲ Walk ID: 148 N. Rudd-Jones

Difficulty rating
Time

▲ Sea, Toilets, National
Trust, Wildlife, Flowers, Great Views

Mewslade Bay from Rhossili

This is a glorious walk combining cliffs with wild beaches and a bird's-eye view of the Gower peninsula from Rhossili Down. If conditions are right, you can visit the enticingly named Worms Head.

1 Turn left onto the path by the visitor centre. Go through the gate and head left towards Worms Head. When the path curves left, cross the grass to the building ahead. Take the grassy path to the southern cliffs. You will soon reach a corner of dry-stone wall on the left – keep alongside it.

2 Turn right just before the gate at the corner of the wall; turn left and follow the wall again. At the next corner turn left. At the junction continue uphill. At the top follow the path along the wall. Continue along the cliff, keeping the wall on your left. Ignore the path to the right above Fall Bay. On reaching a ladder over the wall, do not climb it – follow the middle path. Take the steep path next to the wire fence. Follow the wall towards Mewslade Bay.

3 At the sharp cliffs, head away from the wall. At what looks like a deserted stone shepherd's hut, head uphill. As the white house comes into view to the right, take the grassy path inland.

4 Take the right-hand path opposite the rocky outcrop. Do not cross the stile, but turn right. Continue uphill on the left-hand side of the path. Go through the gate into the woods. Pass through a farm and turn left onto a road. Turn right at the larger road and immediately left at the post box. At the fork take the left track past a house called Bramwood.

5 100 m before the large white house, climb the stile into the Nature Reserve. Follow the path across a footbridge, pass a house on the left, then another stile, to go uphill. Climb the stile and cross a minor road to take the track opposite. Skirt around the reservoir and follow the track left to Rhossili Down. At the fork stay on the wider track to the right to reach a trig point with spectacular views.

6 Retrace your steps for 50 m then take the right fork to Rhossili village. At the corner of the wall, head straight on. At the next corner take the path downhill to the gate. Follow the track. Just before St Mary's Church, take the path to the right. Follow the road to the car park.

access information

The walk starts from the car park at Rhossili, at the end of the B4247 west of the A4118.

Buses 18, 18A, 18C, 18D run to Rhossili from Swansea; call First Cymru for information on 0870 6082608.

Halfway around this circular footpath, you will be rewarded with beautiful views over Mewslade Bay.

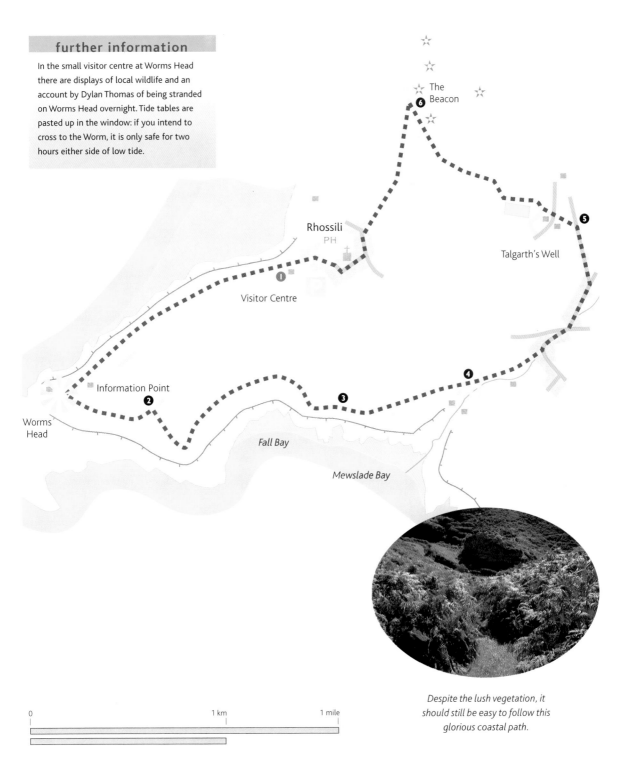

The Beacon ⑥

Rhossili
PH

Talgarth's Well

① Visitor Centre

Information Point ②

Worms
Head

③

④

⑤

Fall Bay

Mewslade Bay

| 0 | 1 km | 1 mile |

*Despite the lush vegetation, it
should still be easy to follow this
glorious coastal path.*

▲ Map: Explorer OL 36
▲ Distance: 1.5 km/1 mile
▲ Walk ID: 1089 Peter Salenieks

Difficulty rating   Time

▲ Sea, Toilets, National Trust, Wildlife, Birds, Flowers, Great Views, Gift Shop, Mostly Flat, Public Transport, Ancient Monument

Martin's Haven & Marine Nature Reserve

This is a scenic circuit of the headland at Martin's Haven, offering views of Skomer Island and Skokholm Island and opportunities for watching seals within the Marine Nature Reserve.

❶ Exit the National Trust car park at the far corner. Walk down a few steps, then turn left and follow the road downhill towards Martin's Haven. Just before the road bends right, go through the kissing gate and turn left. Follow a grassy path, which runs parallel to the stone wall, until you see a stile near the cliff edge, overlooking Deadman's Bay.

❷ The path leads clockwise around the tip of the Marloes Peninsula. After the path bears around to the right, a natural arch can be seen, connecting two coves on the edge of the peninsula. About 200 m after the arch, the path joins a footpath, which leads to Wooltack Point, the northern tip of the peninsula.

❸ Retrace your route from Wooltack Point and bear left, following the footpath along the northern edge of the peninsula, before bearing right and climbing a small hill to reach the old coastguard lookout.

❹ Continue along the footpath until you reach steps leading down to the kissing gate. Go through the kissing gate and follow the road back uphill, passing Lockley Lodge Information Point, to reach the National Trust car park.

access information

The National Trust car park at Martin's Haven is accessible by road from Haverfordwest via the B4327 and a minor road through Marloes.

Martin's Haven can also be reached by the Puffin Shuttle Bus Service 400, which operates between St David's and Milford Haven.

This footpath offers both rugged cliff views and a chance to spot grey seals.

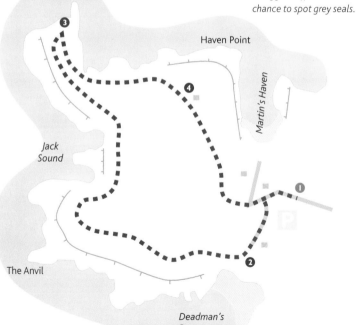

▲ Map: Explorer OL 35
▲ Distance: 7 km/4¼ miles
▲ Walk ID: 1411 Pat Roberts

Difficulty rating

Time

▲ Sea, Toilets, Wildlife, Birds, Flowers, Great Views, Butterflies, Woodland

Witches Cauldron from Moylgrove

This walk is a lovely mixture of coast and countryside, taking in two woodland areas.

At the evocatively named Witches Cauldron, the sea can be quite calm or spectacularly rough.

1 From the car park walk right along the road towards St Dogmaels. Follow the road as it climbs. Where the road swings sharply right, look for a gate on the left. Pass through the gate and walk down through Cwm Trewyddel, following the stream. The path goes over a small bridge and up to join the minor road from Moylgrove.

2 Follow the road round the bend and up the hill for about 120 m. Follow the 'Coast Path' sign on the right, and continue with the sea on your right.

3 Pwll y Wrach (The Witches Cauldron) is a classic example of marine erosion. The path drops right down and climbs sharply back up, passing over a natural arch on the way. The sea comes in under the arch, creating the 'boiling cauldron'. Follow the path down the steps and back up the other side.

4 After the climb you come to a double stile. Leave the coast by the left-hand stile. The route continues over fields initially. After passing a ruined building, enter the woodland of Cwm Ffynnon-alwm to emerge over a stile and turn left onto a green track. This soon becomes a stony farm track climbing gradually.

5 Continue through a gate opposite Treriffith Farm where the sign points right, past the farm buildings then left up the drive. Emerge through a gate and continue to reach the Moylgrove road.

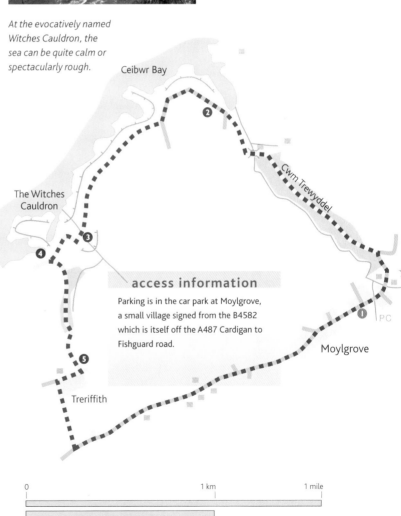

access information

Parking is in the car park at Moylgrove, a small village signed from the B4582 which is itself off the A487 Cardigan to Fishguard road.

▲ Map: Explorer OL 35
▲ Distance: 9 km/5½ miles
▲ Walk ID: 976 D. J. Martin

Difficulty rating

Time

▲ Sea, Toilets, National Trust, Birds, Flowers, Great Views, Café, Food Shop, Ancient Monument

Around St David's Head

This circular walk around St David's Head includes part of the Pembrokeshire Coast Path. There is a short optional diversion from the Coast Path onto Penllechwen Head, which gives extensive coastal views.

1 Leaving the car park, walk up the road, past the first turn on the left. At a marker on the right, turn left up a road. At the top, follow the main track right, towards Upper Porthmawr. After about 100 m the track turns left. Continue past the farmhouse.

2 Above the farmhouse the main track turns left. At this point, just before a small quarry, follow the path off to the right, taking in excellent views of Whitesands Bay, Ramsey Island and St Bride's Bay. At the T-junction, turn right through the gate.

3 A short distance downhill the main track continues straight on, but the walk turns left, behind a low building at a three-way marker, and immediately crosses a stile with another marker. Continue along the bottom of the field, keeping the stone wall on your right, and cross a stile. The next stile, near a farmhouse, crosses onto a track. Turn left to go to the top of the ridge. At the gate follow the track round to the right. Follow the public footpath indicated by the marker. Where the path becomes indistinct, head left of the hill and aim for a gate and stile in the top right of the field. Cross the stile and continue towards a marker.

4 Turn right and follow the track downhill, passing through a metal gate. When you reach a wooden gate, turn to the left onto a grassy track at the bottom of the field. Keep the fence on your right, ignoring side tracks.

5 At the T-junction, turn left up the hill, with a stone wall on your right. The path continues uphill and then between rocky outcrops. Descend towards the sea.

6 When you reach the Pembrokeshire Coast Path, turn left. Keep to the track that is closest to the coast. At Porthmelgan climb up the wooden steps on the path and continue back to Whitesands Bay.

access information

Take the B4583 from St David's towards Whitesands Bay. Whitesands Bay car park is at the end of this road.

A picturesque spot on the Pembrokeshire Coast Path is home to the St Justinian's lifeboat station, which serves the St David's Head area.

Markers point the way along the Coast Path to make navigation extremely easy.

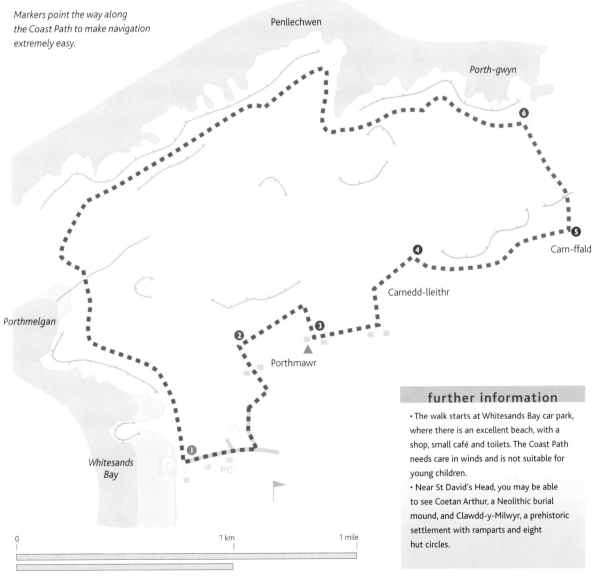

Penllechwen

Porth-gwyn

❻

Carn-ffald
❺

❹
Carnedd-lleithr

Porthmelgan

❷   ❸
Porthmawr

Whitesands Bay

❶

P
PC

0   1 km   1 mile

further information

• The walk starts at Whitesands Bay car park, where there is an excellent beach, with a shop, small café and toilets. The Coast Path needs care in winds and is not suitable for young children.
• Near St David's Head, you may be able to see Coetan Arthur, a Neolithic burial mound, and Clawdd-y-Milwyr, a prehistoric settlement with ramparts and eight hut circles.

▲ Map: Explorer OL 35
▲ Distance: 7 km/4¼ miles
▲ Walk ID: 1414 Pat Roberts

Difficulty rating

👣👣👣

Time

⚫⚫

▲ Sea, Pub, Toilets, Wildlife, Birds,
Flowers, Great Views, Butterflies,
Waterfall, Woodland

Cwm Rhigian Woods from Parrog

Walk part of the Pembrokeshire Coast Path, and enjoy the wildlife in Cwm Rhigian Woods, before walking open moorland and returning to Newport and Parrog.

❶ From the car park, join the coast path by going down the slipway and left, with the sea on your right. If the tide is in, keep above the sea wall and follow the 'High Tide Route' as signed. Follow the Coast Path for over 2 km. Pass the old lifeboat station and Cat Rock. There is lovely scenery to enjoy here, and plenty of sea birds to look out for.

❷ As you drop down into the cove at Aber Rhigian, cross the stream using the footbridge and follow the footpath away from the sea. Soon recross the stream so that it is now on your right-hand side. The stream cascades down and just after a good waterfall, the path swings left, and over another footbridge. Emerge from the wood over a stile, and at a bungalow turn left up the drive. When you reach a T-Junction with another track, turn right up to the A487. Head left for 200 m.

❸ Turn right up the drive to the Hendre. After the farmhouse, go through a gate and carry onto cross a stream. Follow the sign along the left hedge of this field to another stile. Continue straight on up the track, keeping to the right of the hedge to reach a broken stile. Go straight on.

❹ Climb over the stile and continue on up ahead to a wall, which you keep on your right-hand side to soon walk between two walls. Cross a minor road

and continue past a house and through a small gate onto open moorland. Take the left path at the signpost. When you reach the next fork, keep left to continue down a road and over, turning left over a cattle grid towards Newport.

❺ Emerge at the bottom of Mill Lane and take the short cut up the side of the church to reach the A487 at Newport. Head left for 120 m and take the signed road down to the right to the start of the walk at Parrog.

It is possible to see across Newport Sands to St Brynach's Church, home to a 4-metre, elaborately patterned Celtic cross, believed to be the finest in Wales.

further information

While walking down the long descent into Newport, notice the mill stream down on the right side of the road, and the remains of Castle Mill next to the bridge near the bottom.

access information

Park in Parrog car park, at the yacht club. Parrog is signed from the A487 in Newport.

A good bus service serves Newport from Fishguard or Cardigan.

The area is renowned for its scenery and birdlife, and at low tide it is a joy to geologists.

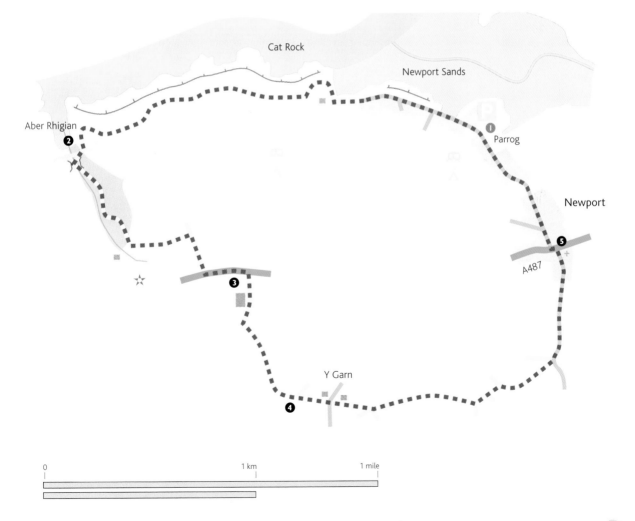

▲ Map: Explorer OL 12
▲ Distance: 9.5 km/6 miles
▲ Walk ID: 1499 John Thorn

Difficulty rating

Time

▲ Hills or Fells, River, Pub, Wildlife, Birds, Great Views, Butterflies, Industrial Archaeology, Moor, Public Transport, Waterfall, Woodland

Hepste Waterfalls from Pontneddfechan

This walk gives a taste of the 'Waterfall Country' south of Ystadfellte — including Sgwd yr Eira where you can walk under the falls — with some moorland sections and great views.

1 From the car park, walk back over the bridge. After 30 m turn sharp right in front of the houses onto a gravel track. Continue along the track, ignoring turns left and right. Opposite the ruins of the Gunpowder Works cross the footbridge. Go straight ahead up a narrow path, and continue up some steps. Turn left at the signs towards Sgwd yr Eira, going through a gate and following the path between spruce trees.

2 Turn right following the 'Advised Path' signs, then left after about 50 m.

3 Turn left at the signpost to Sgwd yr Eira. The path drops steeply down some steps and then there is a short, rocky section before the falls. You can walk under the falls here. Retrace your steps back to the signpost, then follow the signs to Penderyn.

4 Bear right up the hill, keeping the fence on your left. Look out for views to the tops of the Brecon Beacons on your left. Just over the crest of the hill, cross a stile on your left but continue in the same general direction downhill for 50 m to cross another stile. Follow the well-defined track, passing some quarries on your right. Pass a stile on your left and follow the wide track (an old railway). Go through a kissing gate and follow the lane to the road. Turn right onto the road and go steeply uphill, passing a children's playground.

5 Continue ahead, ignoring a junction on your left, and follow the road downhill. Where the road turns left, go straight ahead through a gate. Follow this track for about 1.5 km.

6 The path descends past some old workings on the right and crosses a shallow valley. Ignore the path on your left and follow the path ahead. Continue down to the starting point.

On this walk the tranquility of the countryside contrasts with the thunderous roar of the waterfalls.

access information

This walk starts at the 'waterfalls' car park in Pontneddfechan. Turn off the A465 at the A4109 junction then turn right at the lights. The X5 bus service from Swansea goes to the car park.

It is possible to walk behind the wall of rushing water formed by the Sgwd yr Eira waterfalls.

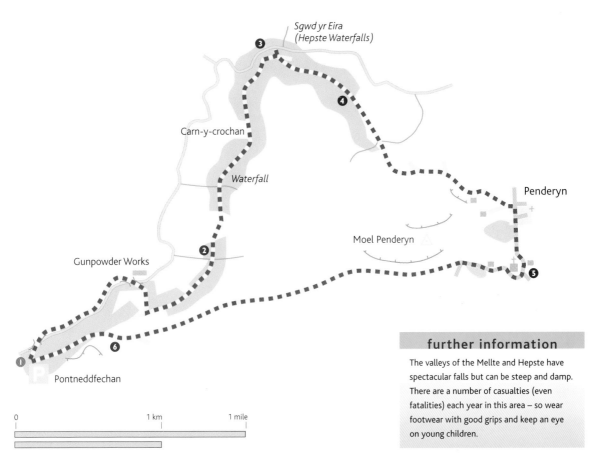

Sgwd yr Eira
(Hepste Waterfalls)

❸

❹

Carn-y-crochan

Waterfall

Penderyn

Moel Penderyn

❷

❺

Gunpowder Works

❻

❶

Pontneddfechan

0   1 km   1 mile

further information

The valleys of the Mellte and Hepste have spectacular falls but can be steep and damp. There are a number of casualties (even fatalities) each year in this area – so wear footwear with good grips and keep an eye on young children.

▲ Map: Explorer OL 20
▲ Distance: 5 km/3 miles
▲ Walk ID: 1131 Dennis Blackford

Difficulty rating

Time

▲ Hills or Fells, Sea, National Trust/
NTS, Wildlife, Birds, Flowers, Great
Views, Butterflies, Public Transport

Man Sands from Sharkham Head

This is an easy-to-follow circular walk that follows tracks and quiet Devonshire country lanes to Man Sands before returning to Sharkham Head along the beautiful South West Coast Path.

❶ From the far end of the car park, cross the stile and follow the grit track. After about 100 m, at the first bend, take the path off to the right. Follow the path through a pair of stone gateposts (it can be muddy at times).

❷ At the end of the path, turn right and follow the farm track.

❸ The track exits into a country road through South Bay Holiday Camp before joining the road to the car park. Turn left onto the road for about 50 m and, immediately past the entrance to the holiday camp, go up the path to the right of the wall. The path widens to become a farm track. Follow the track uphill until arriving at a T-junction. Turn left.

❹ The track ends at a country road. Turn left to follow the road. After about 800 m, the road ends at Southdown Barns. To the left of the gates to a large house join a wooded lane leading downhill to Man Sands. About 500 m down, where the lane bends to the right, continue on down the smaller path off the bend.

❺ The path now leads out on the grass area above the beach. After spending time at the beach, take the coast path up the steep hill to the left.

❻ After about 2 km the path goes over a stone stile into a field. Continue along the coast side of the field. At the end of the field, go over the wooden stile and turn left through the gap, which will lead back to the car park.

Sharkham Head is a site of Special Scientific Interest.

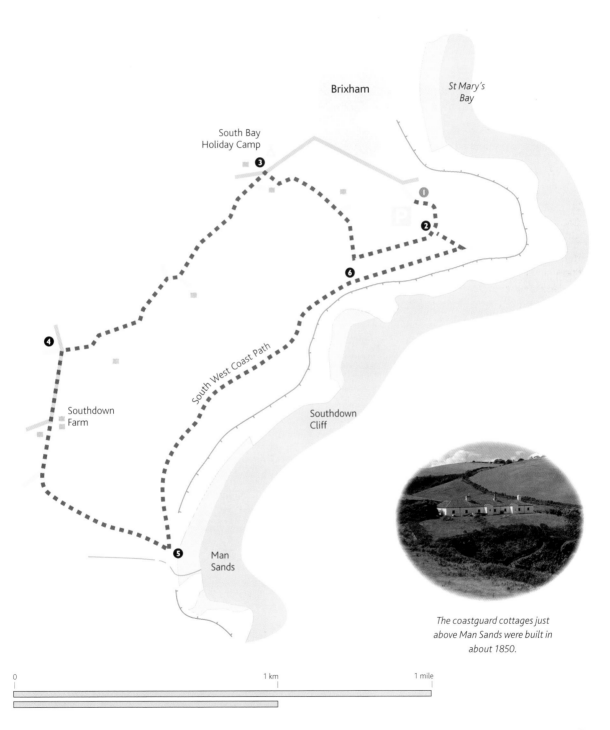

Brixham

St Mary's
Bay

South Bay
Holiday Camp

❸

❶

❷

❻

❹

South West Coast Path

Southdown
Farm

Southdown
Cliff

❺ Man
Sands

*The coastguard cottages just
above Man Sands were built in
about 1850.*

0   1 km   1 mile

▲ Map: Explorer OL 20
▲ Distance: 4 km/2½ miles
▲ Walk ID: 995 Dennis Blackford

Difficulty rating

Time

Hills or Fells, Sea, Wildlife, Birds,
Flowers, Great Views, Butterflies,
Industrial Archaeology

Scabbacombe Coast – Two Bays Walk

This is another pleasant walk taking in part of the South West Coast Path and visiting the two bays of Man Sands and Scabbacombe Sands. It is a fairly short walk, so you will have plenty of time to relax on the beach if you wish.

① Leave the car park and turn right into the road. Follow the road down about 1 km to Man Sands car park. Continue past Man Sands car park. The tarmac road now continues as a stony track. As you near the beach, the path branches to the right. Continue straight on to Man Sands Beach. Return to the branch and walk up a side-shoot for about 100 m to reach a stile on your right. The stone structure that you pass on the way to the beach is an old limekiln where lime was baked to make fertilizer.

② Go into the field via the stile. The path is clearly signposted and passes behind the old coastguard cottages. Walk up the path and through the gap in the wall.

③ Take the path up the hill to the top of the field. Walk south along the South West Coast Path, bearing around to your right and along to the gate.

④ Pass through the gate or over the stile and follow the coast path for about another kilometre to reach another gate and stile.

⑤ After passing through the gate, continue along the coast path for about 400 m until you come to a stile over the fence, leading to Scabbacombe Beach. After spending some time on the beach, return up the path to the stile. Walk back along the coast about 200 m and slightly up to the left, until you come to an isolated stile with no fence. Turn left here and follow the sheep path to the main gate leading into the farm track.

⑥ Pass through the gate or over the stile onto the farm track. At the top of the farm track, pass the large gate and go through the kissing gate back to the car park.

access information

By car, take the Brixham to Kingswear road. About 1.6 km from the small roundabout and restaurant, halfway down a hill past the holiday camp, turn left, signposted 'Kingston, Boohay, Woodhuish and Brownstone'. After about 1.5 km, this lane branches into two lanes with dead-end signs. Take the left-hand one. Just under 1 km away, an opening in the hedgerow on the right leads into the car park.

By bus, take the Brixham to Kingswear bus to the end of the above lane. It is about 2 km from the bus stop to the car park.

further information

The left-hand end of Scabbacombe is a 'clothes optional' beach.

Scabbacombe has a rugged coast.

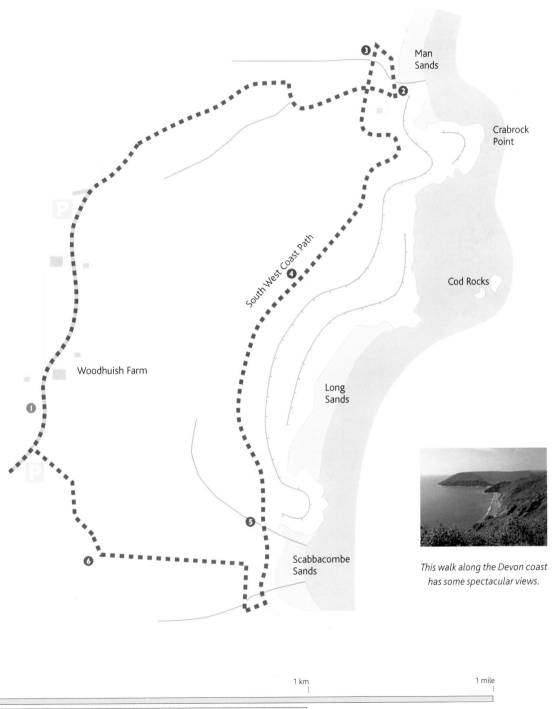

Man Sands

Crabrock Point

South West Coast Path

Cod Rocks

Woodhuish Farm

Long Sands

Scabbacombe Sands

❶ ❷ ❸ ❹ ❺ ❻

This walk along the Devon coast has some spectacular views.

0   1 km   1 mile

▲ Map: Explorer 106
▲ Distance: 11 km/6¾ miles
▲ Walk ID: 699 Pete Brett

Difficulty rating
👣👣👣

Time
●●●

▲ Sea, Pub, Toilets, Museum, Church, Stately Home, Wildlife, Flowers, Great Views, Food Shop, Good for Kids, Tea Shop

South West Coast Path from Padstow

further information

• The Elizabethan manor house of Prideaux Place has a deer park and is open to visitors in summer.
• The church of St Petroc, dating mainly from the 15th century, and the Shipwreck Museum can both be found in Padstow.

This is a circular walk from the Cornish fishing port of Padstow, with long stretches of sandy beach ideal for swimming, and dramatic cliff-top views.

1 Leave the car park on the path to the left of the toilet block and descend to the north side of the harbour. Join the South West Coast Path, which starts near the tourist information centre. The path ascends to the War Memorial with extensive views back towards Padstow and the Camel Estuary. Follow the path around Gun Point to the beautiful sandy Harbour Cove.

2 Cross the sands to rejoin the path. At Hawker's Cove the path joins a short stretch of track behind the beach and skirts the old lifeboat house and terraced pilots' houses.

3 Ascend from the pilots' houses over the stile and take the right path to Stone Daymark. Continue on the coast path above dramatic cliffs with outstanding views.

4 At the stile, turn left inland to reach a road. Follow the road to the village of Crugmeer and curve round to the left at the junction. Pass the cottages on the left and take the next left turn.

5 Take the footpath on the right, just past Little Crugmeer Farm. Cross the stile into the field. Cross diagonally over seven fields with slate stiles to a stile leading onto the road. Turn right along the road and under the arch to Prideaux House. Continue down the road and turn left at the hotel into Fentonluna Lane. Descend through the town to the harbour. From the harbour return to the start via the road.

access information

Follow the A39 south from Wadebridge then take the A389 to Padstow. Do not descend into the town but continue for 200 m and turn into the top car park.

The extent of the fishing port of Padstow is apparent in this aerial view.

0   1 km   1 mile

Difficulty rating

Time

● ● ●

▲ Hills or Fells, Sea, Toilets, Castle, National Trust, Wildlife, Birds, Flowers, Great Views, Butterflies, Restaurant, Tea Shop, Monument

Tintagel Castle and Coast

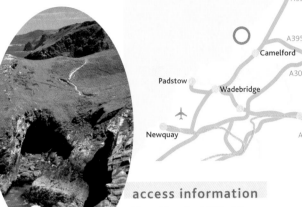

With natural and man-made rock formations, it is no wonder Tintagel is a place of legends.

This walk goes through Tintagel and along the cliff path to visit the legendary castle of King Arthur and Merlin's Cave, with wonderful views and a wealth of wildlife.

1 From the car park, turn right onto the main road and walk into Tintagel village. Walk through the village until reaching the No Through Road at the side of the Cornishman's Inn. Follow this road down to the car park at the end.

2 Follow the church wall around to the right and onto the coast path, looking out for the ruins of the castle below. Follow the path down.

3 On reaching the paved path to the castle, take the path to your right which zigzags down to the visitor centre. At low tide you can go down to the beach and visit Merlin's Cave.

4 Cross over the bridge and climb the steps to continue on the coast path up the other side of the valley. About 200 m further on, after crossing a little wooden bridge, follow the left-hand path up to Barras Nose, with its spectacular view over the cove and the castle. Continue on the coast path. About 1 km further on, pass through a gate which will lead you to Willapark. Pass through the gap in the wall and take the left-hand fork to the point. Return to the junction and

continue on the path to the right of the gap, heading down into the valley.

5 Take the steps up the other side of the valley and cross the stile down to the track. Turn right to return to the starting point.

access information

Tintagel is on the B3263 off the A39. From Tintagel, take the Boscastle road for about 1 km to Bossiney car park on your left.

There are also bus services to take you to Tintagel.

further information

At point 5, instead of turning right, you could turn left to detour down into a secluded cove of Bossiney Haven, which is popular for swimming at low tide.

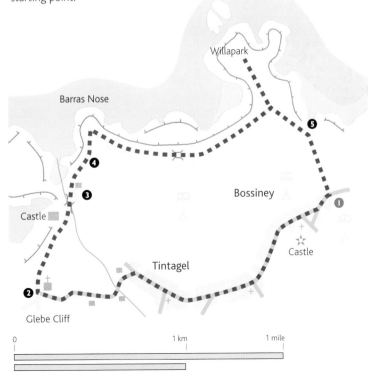

▲ Map: Explorer 105
▲ Distance: 7 km/4¼ miles
▲ Walk ID: 1513 Jim Grindle

Difficulty rating

Time

▲ River, Toilets, Stately Home, National Trust, Wildlife, Birds, Good for Kids, Nature Trail, Restaurant, Tea Shop, Woodland, Ancient Monument

Lamouth Creek from Trelissick Garden

You begin by entering the park and dropping down to follow the river through woods to King Harry Ferry. The walk offers open views of the estuary before a gentle climb through the park back to the start.

❶ Take the path next to the car park, signposted 'Woodland Walks'. Go through a gate next to a cattle grid and follow the path to a junction. Turn right onto the driveway and continue to the edge of a wood.

❷ Go through the gate to the left of the cattle grid, then turn to the right on a path going uphill. Pass the lodge and go through the green gate. Cross the road and go through the gate on the other side. Follow a gravel track that zigzags downhill. When it straightens out there is a stream on the left.

❸ Turn left and cross the stream. On the other side take the right fork, following Lamouth Creek, which is below you on your right. Continue as the woods thin out, until you reach the entrance to the next wood, marked by two low stone banks. Take the right fork, heading over the ditch and then straight through the rampart of the Iron Age fort before joining another track. Turn right. Just before the quay, go down a few steps and emerge into the open.

❹ Visit Roundwood Quay, then retrace your steps back to point 3. Continue with the river now on your left for 1.5 km. You will reach a steep flight of steps leading down to the road you crossed earlier. The ferry is just to your left, and opposite is a white house with a flight of steps going up on its right.

❺ At Bosanko's Cottage, take the track that continues on the far side. Only one track branches off to the right away from the river and your way is signposted. About 1.5 km from the ferry you leave the woods by a kissing gate. Go up the hill, keeping the iron fence on your right.

❻ At the top cross the drive which enters Trelissick House. You will soon reach the exit from the car park. Go through the gate and back to the start.

access information

Trelissick is 6 km south of Truro on the B3289, east of the A39. Buses T7 and 89B run from Truro, where there is a railway station.

This footpath will lead you past cosy woodland cottages to the much grander residence of Trelissick House.

further information

• The first house was built here in about 1750 and went through many hands, with much development of the gardens which were acquired by the National Trust in 1955.

• Roundwood Quay was built in the 18th century to ship tin and copper, and in past days there were buildings for smelting and refining and many wharves. There was a malt house, limekilns and ship-building yards, a busy place compared to the tranquillity that you will find there now.

• Since 1888 the King Harry Steam Ferry Company has operated a ferry which pulls itself across the Fal by chains, but the motive power is now diesel. It is thought that a ferry has existed here since the Norman Conquest.

Roundwood Quay

Woodland Walk

Trelissick

King Harry Ferry

Gardens

0   1 km   1 mile

Hengistbury Head from Christchurch

The route of this popular walk takes in historic Hengistbury Head, a nature reserve and the beach at Sandspit. There are lovely views over Christchurch Harbour and across to the Isle of Wight.

❶ Start with the Ranger Office and Land Train terminus behind you and walk left about 50 m along the road until you reach a junction with the track just before the Double Dykes. Bear right and go along the track. At end of the Double Dykes turn left and follow a path that goes along the cliff-top heading towards Hengistbury Head. Continue past Barn Field and two paths on your left. Climb steadily, keeping the wildlife pond on your right, to reach the top of Warren Hill. Walk along a gravel track, past the coastguard lookout station and, later, a junction on the left.

❷ At the crossroads turn left and follow the track along the cliff-top, passing the southern end of the wildlife pond in the old quarry on your left. Follow the track to the southern tip of Hengistbury Head, before turning left to reach broad steps that lead down to the beach.

Hengistbury Head is a magnificent setting for a footpath. It has a variety of wildlife as well as a wealth of ancient archaeological sites.

further information

Hengistbury Head has witnessed 11,000 years of human history, including a Stone Age camp on Warren Hill, an Iron Age port and 18th-century quarrying. Today it is a popular tourist spot, including a nature reserve, which is home to a variety of birds, insects and small mammals.

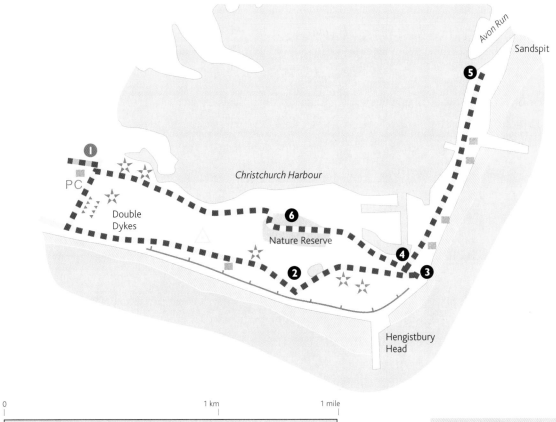

Christchurch Harbour

Avon Run

Sandspit

❺

PC

Double
Dykes

Nature Reserve

❻

❹

❸

❷

Hengistbury
Head

```
0                    1 km              1 mile
|                     |                   |
```

❸ Descend the steps and bear left to pick up a broad path, which leads inland from the beach huts at Sandspit, until you reach the road.

❹ Turn right and follow the road towards Sandspit. Pass the Land Train terminus and the pontoon for the ferry to Mudeford Quay on your left. When you reach the Hut Café, cross between it and the beach office to reach the seaward side of Sandspit and walk towards the end of the spit, where Avon Run marks the outflow from Christchurch Harbour into the sea.

❺ Retrace your route from Avon Run and head right along the road, passing Holloway's Dock, which is a Site of Special Scientific Interest, on your right. Pass a track on your left before entering woodland. Continue until you see a wooded track on your left which leads gently uphill.

❻ Follow the track uphill for about 1 km, reaching the road to return to your starting point.

access information

Cars can be parked in Hengistbury Head car park. This is approached from the A35, turning south onto the B3059 and then east onto the Broadway to the west of Tuckton.

Hengistbury Head is also accessible by bus during the summer. Open Top Coastal Service 12 runs between Sandbanks and Christchurch Quay from the end of May to the end of September. Telephone Yellow Buses (01202) 636060 for further information or visit www.yellowbuses.co.uk.

▲ Map: Explorer 102
▲ Distance: 6.5 km/4 miles
▲ Walk ID: 124 Colin Ward

Difficulty rating

Time

▲ Sea, Pub, Great Views

Lamorna Cove from Mousehole

This walk takes you from the picturesque fishing village of Mousehole to Lamorna, returning along the South West Coast Path.

❶ From the harbour, take the lane past the Lobster Pot restaurant to the Methodist chapel. Walk up the hill, out of the village, to the point where it bears to the right. Keep on the road for about 100 m, and follow the footpath sign to take a path on the left.

❷ Turn right into the field and walk round the edge, until you reach the stile on the far side. Continue walking across the field to reach the farm at Kemyel Drea. The path passes to the right of the first building, and then between the large sheds. Once through the farm, follow the hedge and pick up the path that leads into the hedges beyond.

❸ Walk to the stile and turn left. Continue straight up the lane past the farmhouses, and the gate marked with a Caravan Club sign. Cross the stile, and continue across the fields to the farmhouses of Kemyel Wartha. Follow the track through the hamlet, as it bears right to the footpath sign. Take the path on the left down to the quarry. Continue past the quarry to Lamorna Cove.

❹ Take the obvious path up to Carn-du and continue round the coast for 3 km. Eventually you will come to the road, where you should continue straight on, and down into Mousehole.

further information

• The disused quarry on the way to Lamorna Cove supplied the stone for London Bridge. The cove was once used for shipping the stone, but the difficult task of navigating the harbour rendered it redundant in the last century.
• The South West Coast Path goes through a small wooded nature reserve.

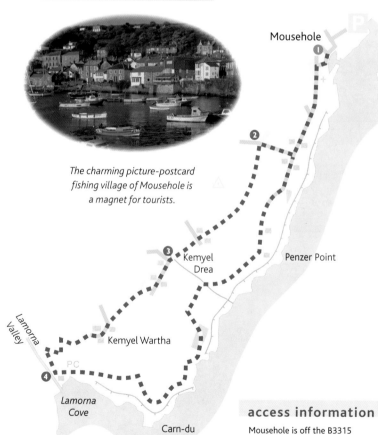

The charming picture-postcard fishing village of Mousehole is a magnet for tourists.

access information

Mousehole is off the B3315 south of the A30 Penzance to Land's End road. Parking is in the village and around the harbour. Buses run from Penzance.

0   1 km   1 mile

▲ Map: Explorer OL 15
▲ Distance: 15 km/9¼ miles
▲ Walk ID: 389 Al Rodger

Difficulty rating

Time

▲ Hills or Fells, Sea, Pub, Toilets, Wildlife, Great Views

Lulworth and White Nothe Coastal Tour

Starting on the ridge above Ringstead, the route first crosses downland to West Lulworth and the magnificent coast at Lulworth Cove and Durdle Door, to return along the cliff-top path.

1 Exit the car park over the stile at the far end and continue down the track. Where the track bears sharp right, cross the stile and continue up the track. Keep straight ahead through two more stiles and a gate.

2 At the second gate, keep straight ahead over the next two rises. As the path rises for a third time, turn right over the stile at the signpost to Newlands Farm Camp Site. Go through Newlands Farm and continue past West Lulworth Church and down to Lulworth Cove.

3 The walk resumes from the pay-and-display car park up Hambury Tout on the stone path, dropping down to the cliff above Durdle Door, then over the small hill to Scratchy Bottom.

4 From Scratchy Bottom cross the stile at the foot of Swyre Head and follow the path diagonally uphill. Cross the stile at the top, to reach a well-used path. Follow the path until reaching the obelisk.

5 At the obelisk, take one of the paths round the hillside and over the summit to the coastguard cottages at the White Nothe. Continue along the cliff-top, with Weymouth Bay in sight ahead. Cross the stile and descend the field onto a track at the next stile.

6 Follow the track uphill, bearing left at a post box. Continue ahead to the car park.

The stretch of coastline between Durdle Door and Lulworth Cove is possibly the most impressive in the whole of Dorset.

access information

This walk starts from the Ringstead Bay National Trust car park on the ridge above Ringstead. Take the Ringstead turning off the A353 between Poxwell and Osmington. Follow the road ahead to the car park, parking towards the far end.

No practical access by public transport.

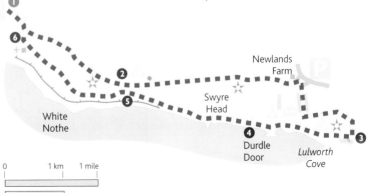

▲ Map: Explorer OL 15
▲ Distance: 10 km/6¼ miles
▲ Walk ID: 365 Al Rodger

Difficulty rating

Time

▲ Sea, Toilets, Church, National
Trust, Wildlife, Birds, Flowers, Great
Views

Old Harry and Ballard Down from Studland

A circular walk from Studland to Old Harry passing Studland's Norman church en route. Continuing up the coast and along the top of Ballard Down, the route returns to Studland via Agglestone Rock.

❶ Exit the car park away from the beach, immediately turning left at the road junction past the car park sign. Turn right at the road junction by the Manor House Hotel. Turn left through the gate and follow the path past St Nicholas's Church and continue straight ahead to the marker post. Turn left down the road and where the road bends left, continue up the track straight ahead to the right of the public toilets. Keep straight ahead to Old Harry, where tracks join at a marker stone.

❷ The route continues up the cliff path. Keep outside the fenced area ahead and pause to sample the views behind you. Continue along the South West Coastal Path. Keep left at the marker stone, taking in the superior views as you go.

❸ At the fence line coming in from the right, bear right away from the cliff and go through the gate and gap in the ancient dyke. Continue along the crest of Ballard Down.

❹ At the obelisk, continue straight ahead through the gate and down the track that bends to the right down to the road. Turn left down the road. Take the path on the right. Go over two stiles and through the woods, straight over the golf course to reach the stile onto the road.

access information

Studland is on the B3351 east of the A351. The walk starts from Middle Beach car park, situated at the end of Beach Road, the northern of the two side roads heading towards the beach.

A bus runs hourly from Bournemouth to Swanage over the ferry and stops at the end of Beach Road.

This chalk arch and stack form a spectacular view at the heart of Studland Bay.

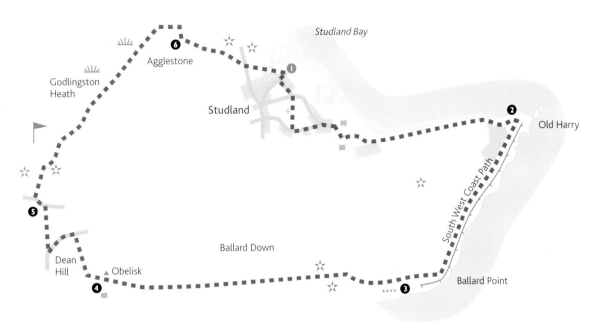

Studland Bay

Agglestone

Godlingston
Heath

Studland

Old Harry

South West Coast Path

Ballard Down

Dean
Hill

Obelisk

Ballard Point

0   1 km   1 mile

The Agglestone Rock
(composed of sandstone
in an area of limestone)
is said to have been thrown
by the Devil from the Isle
of Wight at Corfe Castle.

further information

• St Nicholas's Church has been described as 'the most exciting building in Purbeck'. It is Norman, built on the remnants of a Saxon church destroyed by the Danes.

• Old Harry is the large stack at the end of The Foreland. Sea birds abound at The Foreland, as do land species in the nature reserve on the cliff-top. The spot with its views was special enough for the author H.G. Wells to have his ashes scattered here.

• The obelisk at point 4 was brought to Swanage from London as ship's ballast. It was positioned on top of the Bronze Age barrow to commemorate the first piped water supply into Swanage.

• Legend has it that Agglestone Rock was thrown here from the Isle of Wight by the Devil, who was aiming at Old Harry or Corfe Castle.

❺ Meander left and then right. Pass through two gates onto the good path. Keep straight ahead at the first two marker stones making for Agglestone Studland Heath. Turn left onto a bridle path just before the 'No Entry' signs, skirting the edge of the golf course. At the gate continue straight ahead on towards Agglestone. From Agglestone, the route continues down into the valley, ascending the far side before bearing right and descending again. At the main track, turn right downhill. The track turns sharply to the right and crosses a ford.

❻ Continue up the track and through the gate, turning right at the main road. Cross the road and follow the path on the left through the gully to Beach Road. Turn left to return to the car park.

▲ Map: Explorer OL 14
▲ Distance: 5 km/3 miles
▲ Walk ID: 213 Peter Salenieks

Difficulty rating

Time

▲ River, Pub, Toilets, Church, Wildlife, Birds, Great Views, Cafe, Gift Shop, Tea Shop, Woodland

Devil's Pulpit from Tintern Abbey

This is a short walk from the atmospheric, ivy-clad ruins of Tintern Abbey along woodland paths that lead to the Devil's Pulpit, overlooking the Wye Valley. The route follows part of the Offa's Dyke Path.

❶ From the car park opposite Tintern Abbey, walk along a minor road that leads towards the River Wye. Pass the Anchor pub to reach a footpath on the left. Follow the footpath along the bank of the river. After the footpath turns towards Tintern, pass a whitewashed house on the left and continue along a minor road to reach a T-junction with the A466.

❷ Turn right and continue along the pavement, passing a hotel on your left and an art gallery on your right. Continue until you reach a minor road junction on your right, just past the Abbey Mill.

❸ Walk along the minor road towards the River Wye and cross the footbridge. Continue along the footpath, passing another footpath on the right. Follow the path on the left as it leads uphill, with several metal posts at the start. Shortly after it levels off, there is a junction. Take the right-hand path and follow it until you reach another junction marked by a wooden post with a footpath sign.

❹ Take the right-hand path. At the next junction, turn left and follow the footpath uphill. As the gradient levels off, the path bears to the right. Climb the short flight of wooden steps on the left to reach a junction marked by a wooden post with a footpath sign.

❺ Turn right and walk along the track. At the next junction bear left and follow the footpath uphill to reach Offa's Dyke Path. Turn right at the footpath sign and walk along Offa's Dyke Path until you reach a junction and a sign at a right-hand bend.

❻ Continue along Offa's Dyke Path from the footpath sign to reach the Devil's Pulpit. Retrace your route to the start.

The Devil's Pulpit juts out from the cliffs beside Offa's Dyke, high above the River Wye.

access information

Tintern lies between Monmouth and Chepstow in the Wye Valley. The abbey is just off the A466, at the southern end of the village. There is a car park just off the main road. If this is full, the car park for Tintern Abbey is at the rear of the abbey, beside the River Wye.

further information

• This walk can be combined with a visit to Tintern Abbey. Contact the information centre on 01291 689251 for information about when the abbey is open.

• The Devil's Pulpit is a small limestone rock that juts out from the cliffs. It looks down over Tintern Abbey from the hills beside Offa's Dyke on the eastern side of the River Wye. Local legend has it that the Devil stood upon the Devil's Pulpit to preach to the monks below, tempting them to desert their order.

The view of Tintern Abbey from the Devil's Pulpit takes in a vast expanse of the River Wye.

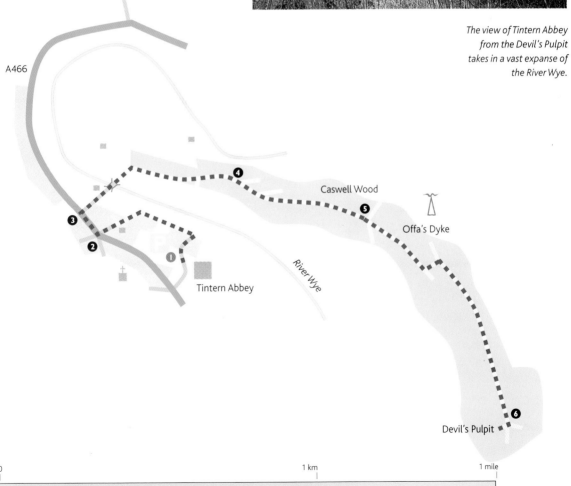

A466

Caswell Wood

Offa's Dyke

River Wye

Tintern Abbey

Devil's Pulpit

0   1 km   1 mile

- Map: Explorer 152
- Distance: 6.5 km/4 miles
- Walk ID: 999 John Thorn

Difficulty rating

Time

Pub, Castle, Birds, Flowers, Great Views, Butterflies, Industrial Archaeology, Public Transport, Woodland, Ancient Monument

Ruperra Castle from Draethen

This is a pleasant walk that follows a route almost entirely through varied woodland, with the added interest of passing the ruins of Ruperra Castle and an Iron Age fort along the way.

1 From the centre of the village walk up the road signposted Rudry and Lisvane. At the bridle path sign, turn right up a concrete drive. At the cottage, turn left to follow the bridleway sign, through a gate, then another gate into the woods. Just after the track levels out turn right at a T-junction, then left. Emerge onto an open area with several paths.

2 Take the gravel track slightly to the left. Almost immediately take a hard-to-see path that drops down steeply to the left. Towards the bottom of the valley, where the path turns right and the woods open out a little, turn left past a ruined cottage. Cross the road by going left then right down a drive marked 'The Retreat'. Go between the houses. Do not turn left into a gate, but cross a gravelled area, go down some steps and cross a footbridge. Take the left-hand path up through the woods. Cross a track and continue. Pass a steel barn on your left, go through the gate and turn left onto a road. Just past a cottage, bear right, keeping the woods on the left and the field on the right.

3 At the end of the field, go through the kissing gate and follow the wall, crossing two stiles. At the end of the wall, turn left to a gateway for a view of Ruperra Castle. Retrace your steps back to the wall, then turn right past the gateway marked 'Ruperra Castle Farm'.

Bear left, slightly uphill, for another view of the castle.

4 Before you reach a gateway, turn left uphill following yellow arrows. When you reach another path, turn right to climb the ridge to the top of the Iron Age hill fort. When the track turns sharp right, follow it down, then left.

5 Turn right at a junction then right at the next junction to return to point 4. Climb away from the wall but continue across the next path, following the arrows. Turn right at a wider track.

6 Turn left onto a narrow path. Continue down through the woodland. Go through a kissing gate into a field. Follow the right-hand side of the field down into the valley. Turn right at the stile to reach the starting point.

further information

As the path levels out at point 4 there are fine views of the castle, Cardiff, the Bristol Channel and the Quantocks.

The original 17th-century castle of Rupera was twice destroyed by fire and was rebuilt once. It is now nothing more than a romantic ruin.

access information

This walk starts in Draethen. In the centre of the village, opposite the post and telephone boxes, turn towards the Hollybush Inn but instead of crossing either of the bridges turn sharp left onto a gravelled area in front of an old stone barn.

Buses from Caerphilly to Newport stop in Lower Machen, on the A468.

Rupera Castle was built to command views across a swathe of countryside.

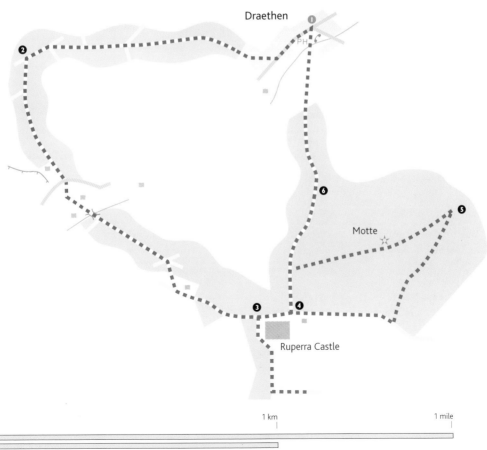

▲ Map: Explorer OL 35
▲ Distance: 11 km/6¾ miles
▲ Walk ID: 1323 Pat Roberts

Difficulty rating
👣👣👣

Time
●●●◖

▲ Mountains, Wildlife, Birds, Flowers, Great Views, Butterflies, Moor, Tea Shop, Woodland

Carningli from Sychbant

This walk climbs to Bedd Morris, then onto Carningli, for incredible views of the Wicklow Hills in Ireland, the Welsh coast and the Preseli Hills, to return down through the Gwaun Valley.

1 From the car park walk up the drive to Ffald-y-Brenin (Sychbant on the map). Where the drive swings left, go over the marked stile to the left of the gate. Continue up a field to pass through another gate. Turn left to reach a gate with blue arrows. Go through the gate and turn right up a green lane. Go over two stiles in quick succession to enter the forest. An information board tells us that this is the 'Penlan Project'. Follow the arrow to the right, to Carningli. After about 1 km bear left towards Bedd Morris and emerge from the forest on a stony track.

2 At Bedd Morris, with the stone behind you, walk ahead on a path that follows a raised bank in an easterly direction, leaving the bank to curve slightly left over the top of Mynydd Caregog. After passing above the forest, a fence comes in from the right. Follow the grassy path, keeping the fence on your right. As you come level with Carn Edward, a large rocky outcrop on the right, take the left fork, then turn immediately left again.

3 Keep heading towards Carningli, following any of the small paths. Once you are within 150 m of the outcrop, head for the northern end, and you will see a well-used route up onto the top.

4 At the top of Carningli there are fantastic views. Retrace your steps off the outcrop, and turn right. Take the most suitable path round the rocks. Descend on the narrow but good path heading east. Follow the path down to the Dolrannog road.

5 On reaching the road turn right. Go through the farmyard and walk through a metal gate to pass Dolrannog Uchaf.

6 At the end of the road go through the gate to the left of the bungalow. Follow the bridle path down through the woods to reach Llanerch and the valley road. Turn right to return to the start.

further information

There are many legends attached to Bedd Morris, but it is most likely a Bronze Age standing stone and is now one of the markers standing on Newport Parish Boundary.

An ancient copper beech tree presides over the Preseli Hills like a monument to the enduring power of nature.

access information

Parking is at the Sychbant Picnic Site on a
minor road off the B4313 out of Fishguard.
Look for the sign for 'Ffald-y-Brenin' at a
bend in the road. This house is marked on
the Ordnance Survey® map as 'Sychbant'
and is next to the car park.

*With its weather-beaten rocks, standing
stones and ancient legends, Carningli is
not a place for the faint-hearted.*

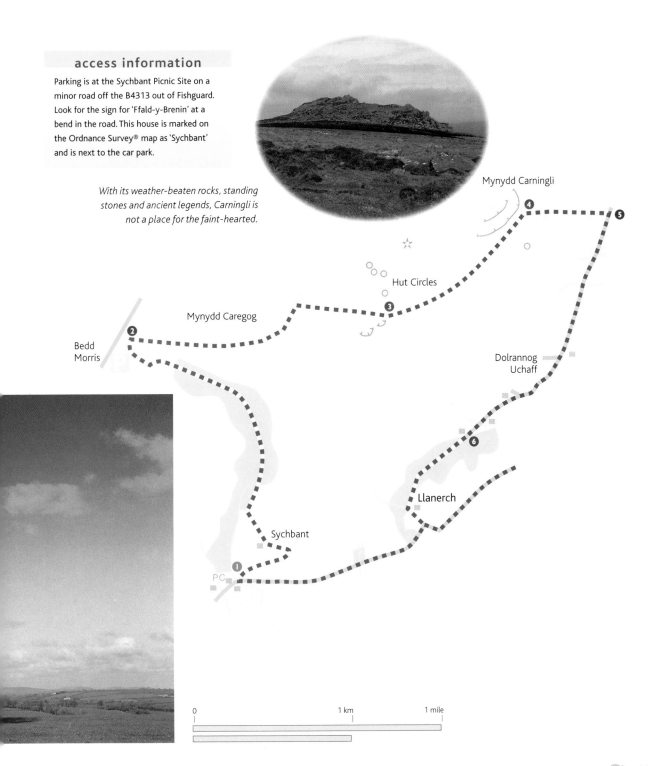

Mynydd Carningli

Hut Circles

Mynydd Caregog

Bedd
Morris

Dolrannog
Uchaff

Llanerch

Sychbant

PC

0   1 km   1 mile

▲ Map: Explorer 200
▲ Distance: 9 km/5½ miles
▲ Walk ID: 951 Pete Brett

Difficulty rating

👣👣👣

Time

⚫⚫⚫

▲ Hills or Fells, Reservoir, Toilets, Play Area, Church, Wildlife, Birds, Flowers, Great Views, Good for Wheelchairs, Nature Trail, Tea Shop, Woodland

Garreg-ddu Reservoir from Elan Valley

This relatively short walk offers the walker peace and tranquillity amidst superb scenery.

❶ Leave the car park taking the ascending path to a cinder track and turn left towards Caban Coch Dam. Remain on the track beside the reservoir until reaching the arched road bridge.

❷ Cross the road by Foel Tower and rejoin the track. (If time permits you can turn left over the road bridge and visit Nantgwyllt Church on the far bank.) Leave the track through the gate and continue on the grass verge beside the road for 200 m to the bridle path on the right. Climb the bridle path steeply at first then over the stream, ignoring any small side tracks.

❸ Where the path branches left, continue straight ahead towards high ground for all-round views. From the viewpoint return to this point and descend the path, following small posts and signs to reach a metal gate.

❹ At the gate turn right and continue to descend, following little yellow markers until you reach a wire fence. Turn left and follow the fence to the gates of the water treatment buildings. Go through the gates and down steps to the road.

❺ Cross the road. Behind the houses, cross the footbridge over the river. Turn right and follow the river through the Elan estate to pass the toilets on the left. Go through a white gate beside the bridges into Cnwch woods and continue on the path through the trees.

❻ Go behind the first turbine house and cross the bridge in front of the dam. Head behind the second turbine house to return to the visitor centre car park.

The bridge over the majestic Caban Coch Dam forms an integral part of this walk.

access information

From Rhayader take the B4518 road heading south-west (follow signs to Elan Valley Reservoirs) and park at the Elan Valley Visitor Centre.

further information

Wheelchair users can follow the route alongside the reservoirs, returning to the visitor centre the same way.

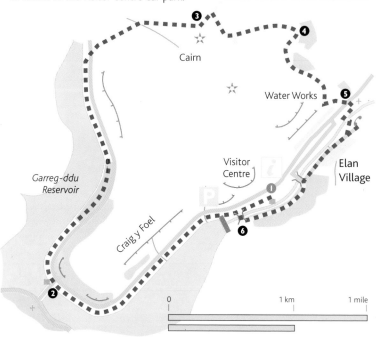

▲ Map: Explorer OL 12
▲ Distance: 11 km/6³/₄ miles
▲ Walk ID: 1290 John Thorn

Difficulty rating

Time

▲ Mountains, Reservoir, National Trust, Wildlife, Birds, Flowers, Great Views

Brecon Beacons Horseshoe

access information
Start at the parking area by the dam of the lower Neuadd reservoir. Access is from the minor road between Vaynor/Merthyr and Talybont off the A465.

This walk to the top of the Brecon Beacons has stupendous views from almost every point.

1 Do not go through the gate but turn up to the right to reach a track. Cross the stile and walk between the two fences. When the fence on your right turns right follow it up. As you approach the trees bear left to join the rough track. Turn left onto the Roman road. Go down a steep dip and up the other side, bearing right. Follow the track to the top of the pass.

2 At the top, cross the stile on your left and bear left on the well-defined path that climbs around the shoulder of Cribyn. At the saddle between Cribyn and Pen y Fan, continue ahead climbing steeply. Look over your right shoulder for views of Cribyn, Llangorse Lake, the Black Mountains and, later, the Sugar Loaf.

3 The summit of Pen y Fan has commanding views in all directions. Descend towards the flat top of Corn Du, but at the saddle bear left. At the next saddle bear left again, climbing slightly to follow the escarpment for about 3 km. You pass to the left of a large cairn, following the edge. Pass another large cairn and ignore the steep path down to your left in a fold in the mountain.

4 Turn right to start a steep descent, aiming for the end of the dam. Go though the gate, walk along the dam then veer off to the right to cross a bridge. Go through the gate to reach the starting point.

The Brecon Beacons.

further information
Pen y Fan (see photo on page 44) is the highest point in South Wales. Do not attempt this walk in poor visibility. Most of the paths on the first part are well defined but less so after leaving Corn Du, and parts of the route can be muddy or boggy.

▲ Map: Explorer OL 13

▲ Distance: 10 km/6¼ miles

▲ Walk ID: 1511 Pat Roberts

Difficulty rating

👣👣👣

Time

●●●◑

▲ Mountains, Pub, Wildlife, Birds, Great Views, Industrial Archaeology, Ancient Monument

Blaenavon from Foxhunter Car Park

This walk in the Blaenavon heritage area takes in a visit to the Ironworks, as well as views of Big Pit and Coity Mountain. The return route is across opencast landscape, past old mines with fine views of the Brecon Beacons and the Black Mountains.

❶ From the car park walk to the minor road by the masts and go right for a short distance. Take the narrow path on the left towards the telegraph poles. Just above a covered reservoir join a gravel path to reach the B4246. Turn left towards Blaenavon. As you reach the 30 mph signs, cross the road.

❷ Opposite the Riflemans Arms, take a path through a car park and picnic area, to emerge on a road. Cross over to reach the footpath and head downhill. Soon take a right turn, just after a left bend, where you can see the ironworks on the right. Just after the bend, go down the steps in front of York House. Cross over to join another road with the ironworks railings on your right. Continue down the road to visit the ironworks.

❸ Head down the hill and take the first turn on the right. Follow this road to join the B4248 road to Brynmawr. Turn left and continue until you reach a bus shelter on your right.

❹ Just past the bus shelter, take the lane up towards two houses. Where the lane swings right, continue ahead on a track. Go over another stepped gate and through another gate to follow the track up into the open hillside.

❺ You will come across a square chimney stack with a tree growing out of the top. To each side you will see fenced-off areas. Continue on the track to reach another fenced square. Ignore a yellow arrow pointing straight on and head for the incline on the right.

❻ At the ridge there are views of Brecon Beacons and the Black Mountains. Take the right-hand path towards the masts. Maintain direction, heading just right of the masts, until you reach the B4246. You should emerge opposite the side-road leading to the masts and car park.

access information

Park at the Foxhunter car park, near the masts on the Blorenge. Take the B4246 road from Abergavenny to Blaenavon, and turn off near the Keeper's Pond at the top, heading for the two big masts. These should also help you to navigate the walk.

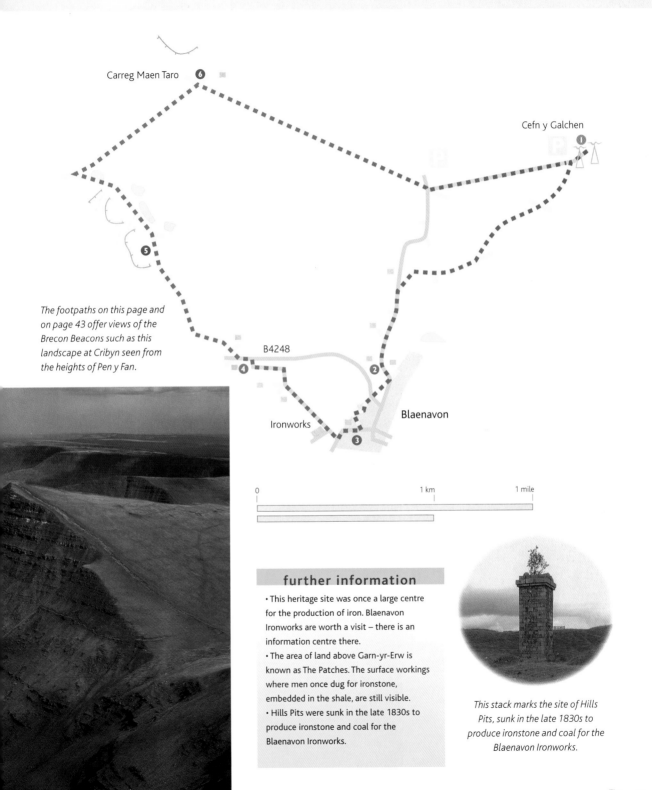

Carreg Maen Taro ⑥

Cefn y Galchen ①

The footpaths on this page and on page 43 offer views of the Brecon Beacons such as this landscape at Cribyn seen from the heights of Pen y Fan.

⑤

④ B4248 ②

Ironworks

Blaenavon

③

0   1 km   1 mile

further information

• This heritage site was once a large centre for the production of iron. Blaenavon Ironworks are worth a visit – there is an information centre there.

• The area of land above Garn-yr-Erw is known as The Patches. The surface workings where men once dug for ironstone, embedded in the shale, are still visible.

• Hills Pits were sunk in the late 1830s to produce ironstone and coal for the Blaenavon Ironworks.

This stack marks the site of Hills Pits, sunk in the late 1830s to produce ironstone and coal for the Blaenavon Ironworks.

Difficulty rating

Time

▲ Mountains, Church, Wildlife, Birds, Flowers, Great Views, Butterflies, Waterfall

Revenge Stone from Pont Esgob

This route combines two ridge walks with a visit to an attractive old church, a memorial stone with a very unusual name, an Iron Age hill fort and a walk in the Grwyne Valley.

❶ Take the minor road signed Patrishow and Crickhowell. Keep right at the fork and follow the road, ignoring the road on the left. Just below the church, approach the Holy Well of St Issui by paving stones on the right.

❷ Walk through the churchyard and through a gate onto the hillside. Join a track, and, above the farmhouse on the right, head right and down, keeping the wall on your left. Pass between the buildings to reach a track. Go through the first gate on the left and cross a field to a stile. Continue down the next field to a stile and then left and down past ruins to reach another stile by the road.

❸ Cross the road and continue down the minor road. Pass the chapel and keep to the road. Keep to the right of the farm and buildings and keep to the main track leading gently upwards. At the farm, keep to the right of the farmhouse to reach a gate, which leads to a sunken stony path. Continue through another gate, keeping to the right wall. As the wall swings right, go straight up to the ridge and the memorial stone.

❹ At Dial Garreg (The Revenge Stone), turn right to walk the ridge. At the fork, take the left path to reach a wide, grassy track, heading towards Twyn y Gaer. As the wall and track start to swing away from the fort, and there is a junction of

paths, continue on the central green track up to the top of Twyn y Gaer.

❺ Retrace your steps down from the top and at a cross paths fork left, keeping to the fence on your left. Cross the stile and head down, across grass and then on an old drovers' road between two old walls.

❻ At a break in the wall, keep to the right of the wall to reach a stile onto another stony track. Continue bearing left and down to join a road, then right and down, eventually to reach the starting point of the walk.

further information

• The Revenge Stone marks the spot where the Norman Marcher Lord, Richard de Clare, was attacked and killed by Morgan ap Owen in 1135.
• Twyn y Gaer is a fine Iron Age fort with extensive views.

Seen here from a point near Crickhowell, Powys, the Black Mountains provide a majestic background to the landscape.

No public transport. Parking is at the roadside, at Five-ways, Pont Esgob. This is on a minor road between Lower Cwmyoy and Forest Coal Pit, off the A465 just north-east of Abergavenny.

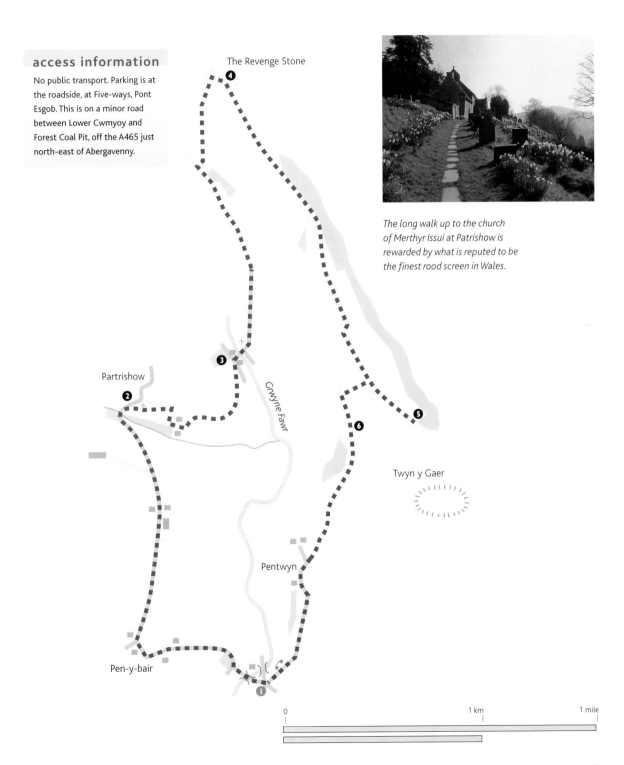

The Revenge Stone

❹

❸

Partrishow

❷

Grwyne Fawr

❺

❻

Twyn y Gaer

Pentwyn

Pen-y-bair

❶

The long walk up to the church of Merthyr Issui at Patrishow is rewarded by what is reputed to be the finest rood screen in Wales.

0		1 km	1 mile

▲ Map: Explorer OL 13
▲ Distance: 8 km/5 miles
▲ Walk ID: 307 Peter Salenieks

Difficulty rating

👣👣

Time

● ● ●

▲ Hills or Fells, Mountains, Pub, Toilets, Church, Great Views

Hatterrall Hill from Llanthony Priory

This is a short circular walk set in the heart of the Black Mountains, with fine views of the surrounding hills and plains. At the start or end of your walk, you can wander among the Gothic arches of the ruined Llanthony Priory.

1 As you leave the car park walk straight ahead, keeping the Abbey Hotel and Llanthony Priory on your right. A short distance ahead, there is a footpath sign next to a gate and a stile. Cross the stile and turn right. Keep the Abbey Hotel on your right and walk for about 100 m.

2 Cross the stile and follow the sign to Offa's Dyke. The footpath leads along a track across a field. Close to a small stream, turn left at the National Park marker and walk a few metres to cross the first of a series of five stiles. The path leads gently uphill across fields towards Loxidge Tump. There is a National Park sign next to the fifth stile, which includes a map of Hatterrall Hill. Now the path climbs through bracken, before bearing right and zigzagging to gain the ridge. Cross open ground along a path, which passes a small cairn before joining Offa's Dyke Path at a milestone (signed Llanthony).

3 Turn right at the milestone and walk along Offa's Dyke Path for about 3 km. The path dips into a col, where another milestone points to Longtown and Llanthony.

4 Turn right and follow the footpath down towards Llanthony, taking in the views of the Vale of Ewyas. Continue for about 1.5 km along this footpath until you reach a junction with a footpath

sign and a stile on the left, together with a National Park sign.

5 Cross the stile and follow the footpath downhill, keeping the fence on your left. Cross another stile and enter Wiral Wood. The footpath bears right then left at a small stream, before crossing another stile at the edge of the woods. Cross the field to a stile in the bottom right corner.

6 Cross the stile and follow the dry-stone wall, keeping Llanthony Priory to your left, until you reach the stile at point 2. Cross the stile and retrace your route to the start.

access information

Approach the start by road from Abergavenny or Hereford along the A465 to Llanvihangel Crucorney. Then follow minor roads for 10 km to reach Llanthony. Park in the free car park at Llanthony Priory.

Abandoned by the Augustinian monks in 1134, Llanthony Priory's ruined skeleton stands forlornly in the shadow of the Black Mountains.

further information

Pony trekking can be arranged at Court Farm, which is immediately adjacent to the Abbey Hotel.

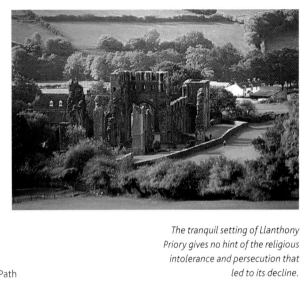

The tranquil setting of Llanthony Priory gives no hint of the religious intolerance and persecution that led to its decline.

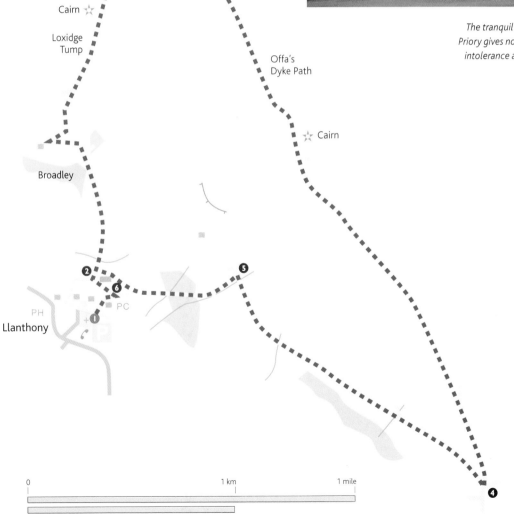

Black Darren

Cairn ☆

Loxidge Tump

Offa's Dyke Path

☆ Cairn

Broadley

Llanthony

PH

PC

0   1 km   1 mile

▲ Map: Explorer 102
▲ Distance: 7 km/4¹/₄ miles
▲ Walk ID: 1038 Dennis Blackford

Difficulty rating
👣👣👣

Time
⬤⬤⬤

▲ Hills or Fells, Lake/Loch, Wildlife, Birds, Flowers, Great Views, Butterflies, Industrial Archaeology, Moor, Ancient Monument

Nancledra

further information

From Roger's Tower there are fine views and you are surrounded by the ancient hill fort of Castle-an-Dinas.

Redruth
St Ives
St Just   A307
A30
Penzance
A394
Helston

This moorland walk to the ancient hill fort of Castle-an-Dinas and Roger's Tower, a folly built in 1798, offers superb views over St Michael's Mount and Penzance bay.

❶ Leave the car park and turn left down the main road to the junction. Turn right and continue up the country road.

❷ Cross a small bridge and turn left at a branch in the road. Look for a house called The Moors and take the farm track to the right of the house. Continue to the top of the hill.

❸ When you reach the junction, take the left-hand track until you come to a large house with a footpath to the right. Follow the path through a gate into a field. Cross the field to another gate in the top-left-hand corner. Pass through the gate into another field and walk straight ahead to another gate leading into a large field.

❹ Cross the field to pass through a pair of gates, turn right onto the track and continue for about 800 m. At the chimney, turn left onto a wide track. Continue past an old engine house. After about 300 m turn right through a break in the wall. Turn left and follow the track round until it ends in a field near a pile of rocks. Cross the field diagonally right to reach a track leading to a gate with a stile. Cross the stile and turn left. Continue up to reach a wide track.

❺ Turn left and stay on the main track, which curves to the left at the new quarry. Go through the gate and walk along the quarry until you arrive at a path leading to Roger's Tower.

❻ Return to the track along the quarry rim and turn left. The track goes though a gateway in a wall and becomes a rough path. At the end of the quarry, head downhill. Go through the gate and bear right across the moor. Continue across a telegraph pole on the ground, through a wide gap in the hedge and onto a farm track. Head to the right towards the farmhouse.

❼ Go through the gate by the farm and turn right, following the road to the main road. Turn left and walk back to the start.

access information

There is a bus service number 16 from St Ives and Penzance stopping in the village.

Nancledra is midway (about 6 km) on the B3311 road from St Ives to Penzance. On entering this small village watch for the tiny post office on the left. Turn up the track a little past the post office, which leads to the village car park.

St Michael's Mount, a former Benedictine priory and castle, is now the home of the St Aubyn family.

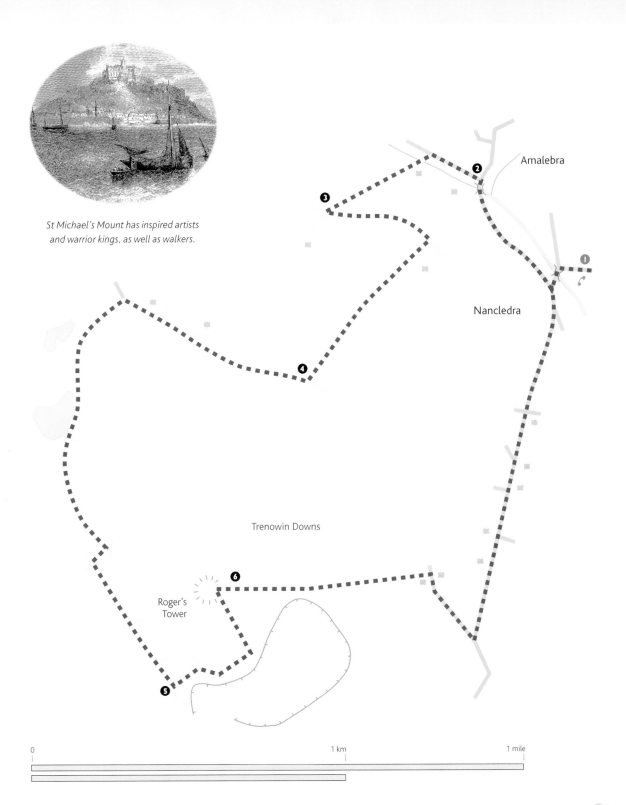

St Michael's Mount has inspired artists
and warrior kings, as well as walkers.

Amalebra

Nancledra

Trenowin Downs

Roger's
Tower

▲ Map: Explorer OL 28
▲ Distance: 15 km/9¼ miles
▲ Walk ID: 1428 Paul Edney

Difficulty rating

Time

▲ Hills or Fells, Pub, Church, Great Views, Café, Moor, Tea Shop, Ancient Monument

Grimspound from Widecombe

This walk from Widecombe takes in the Bronze Age enclosure at Grimspound, and includes spectacular views all along the top of Hamel Down. The route also includes the remains of a medieval village.

1 From the car park, turn right along the path on the other side of the fence. Join the road on the other side of the village green. After 200 m turn left up the path signed Grimspound via Hameldown. Keep right and continue up a stony track. Go through the gate and take the path up the hillside.

2 The wall on your right turns right, where your path joins the Two Moors Way. Turn right and keep to the path just above the wall. Where the wall turns right again, head across open ground. Take either path to the top of Hamel Down. Eventually, just to the left of the path, cross to the trig point at Hameldown Tor. Continue downhill towards Grimspound.

3 In the middle of the compound, turn right and follow the path towards the road at Natsworthy. Go through the gate onto the road, head left for 10 m, then turn right onto the bridle path. Go through the gate where the bridle path meets the road. Go past Jay's Grave, cross the road, continue through the gate opposite onto the bridle path and over the hill.

4 Where the bridle path meets another road, with Bowerman's Nose to the left, turn right and follow the road towards Hound Tor.

5 At the crossroads, turn left and cross the grass to Hound Tor. Go down into the remains of the medieval village. Pick up the path over the shoulder of the hill to the right of Greator Rocks. Go through the right-hand gate in the wall and take the right-hand path to Bonehill Down. At the top go through a gap in the wall and continue on the path downhill. Ignore the path to the left and continue to a gate.

6 Go through the gate and turn left onto the road, down to the river. Cross the cattle grid and head to the right, across the Down. Take the left fork at the junction. Over the rise, Bell Tor is on your right.

7 Join the road and turn right, to reach a T-junction. Turn right to return to Widecombe.

further information

• From the trig point at Hameldown Tor you have a bird's eye view of Grimspound, which is probably the best preserved Bronze Age enclosure on the moor.
• Since 1860, when Kitty Jay's grave was discovered and restored, there have always been fresh flowers on the grave, although no one admits to putting them there.
• Bowerman's Nose is only a few minutes off the route and is worth a visit. Legend has it that the shape is due to a bowman who discovered a coven of witches. They turned him and his hounds to stone. The hounds can be seen at Hound Tor.

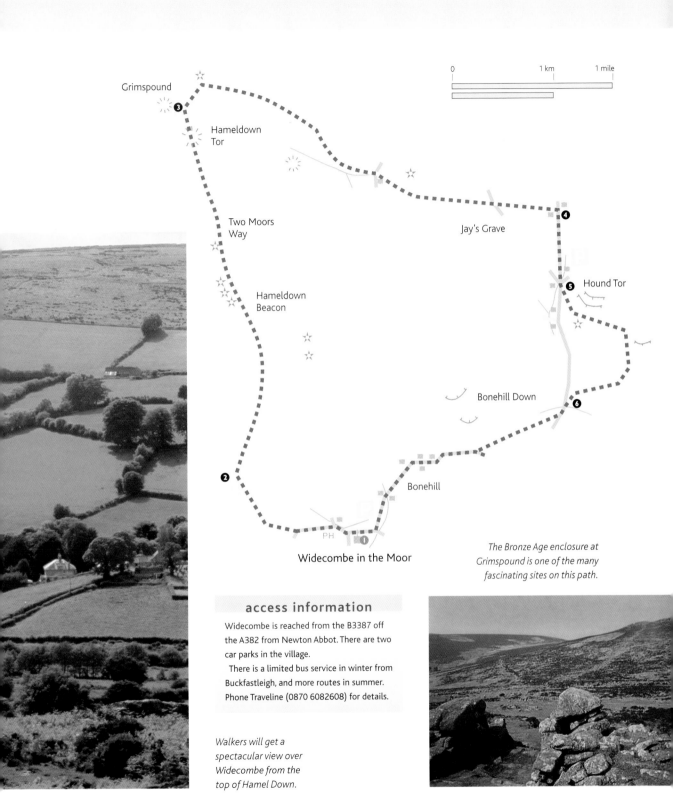

0   1 km   1 mile

Grimspound

❸

Hameldown
Tor

Two Moors
Way

Jay's Grave

❹

Hameldown
Beacon

Hound Tor
❺

Bonehill Down
❻

Bonehill

❷

Widecombe in the Moor

PH
❶

The Bronze Age enclosure at
Grimspound is one of the many
fascinating sites on this path.

access information

Widecombe is reached from the B3387 off
the A382 from Newton Abbot. There are two
car parks in the village.

There is a limited bus service in winter from
Buckfastleigh, and more routes in summer.
Phone Traveline (0870 6082608) for details.

*Walkers will get a
spectacular view over
Widecombe from the
top of Hamel Down.*

▲ Map: Explorer 111
▲ Distance: 3 km/1¾ miles
▲ Walk ID: 1479 Dennis Blackford

Difficulty rating   Time

▲ River, Church, Wildlife, Birds, Flowers, Great Views, Butterflies, Public Transport, Nature Trail, Waterfall, Woodland, Ancient Monument

St Nectan's Glen.

St Nectan's Glen

This circular walk begins from the 6th-century chapel of St Piran and the ancient well, ascending a bridleway to a viewpoint overlooking Tintagel Bay, before descending down into the beautiful wooded valley of St Nectan's Glen.

❶ Start the walk on the public bridleway to the left of the church. Follow this track to the top of the hill.
❷ Go through several gates and follow the track as it turns to the right. As the track descends, look over the hedge to your right for spectacular views of the Tintagel coast. The track ends and a path continues down to the right between the metal gate and the wooden buildings.
❸ At the Hermitage Tea Gardens there is access to a waterfall. After visiting the waterfall, take the path to the right of the gardens, which leads down into St Nectan's Glen. Ignore all other paths and descend the steps. The path levels out and runs along the gorge. The path descends down more steps to reach the valley floor. Continue along the path beside the river. Follow the path across the river by a wooden bridge before crossing back via a concrete one. Where the path branches, ignore the path over the bridge and keep to the right-hand side of the river.
❹ After ascending again, the path emerges onto an access road. Follow the road back to the church.

further information

St Nectan's Well is opposite the small car park at the start of the walk. The well would have dated back many hundreds of years before St Piran's name was attached to it.

access information

Take the B3263 from Tintagel or Boscastle to the Rocky Valley Inn approximately midway between the two, where you will find a concrete bus shelter on the seaward side of the road and a car park near by. By the shelter there is a sign pointing to a rough track leading to St Piran's Church and Well. It also indicates St Nectan's Glen. You can also drive up this track about 250 m to a small car park by the church where the walk begins.

You can take the bus from Tintagel or Boscastle to the Rocky Valley Inn and walk up to the church.

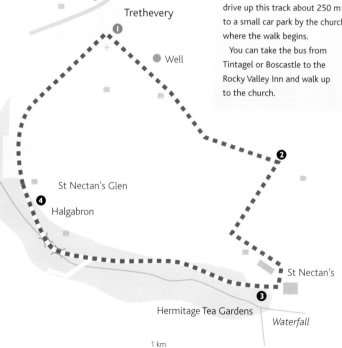

Trethevery

Well

St Nectan's Glen

Halgabron

St Nectan's

Hermitage Tea Gardens

Waterfall

0   1 km   1 mile

Difficulty rating

Time

Fingle Bridge from Chagford

This walk is mostly through woodland along the beautiful Teign Valley, with flowers, views and wildlife, and offers the chance to visit Castle Drogo, an early 20th-century Lutyens country house.

1 From the car park walk up the slight rise, passing a stone cottage on your left. Then turn right to go across the farmyard, bearing slightly left to reach a field. The way across the field is marked by a post. Pass through a gate to cross a second field. Go through the next gate into some woodland. Bear right at a sign marked 'Road at Dogmarsh Bridge'. Cross the A382 and enter the Castle Drogo estate by the kissing gate. Walk through the field with the river on your right.

2 Just after entering the woodlands, cross a stile and turn left following the sign 'Hunter's Path'. Walk uphill to pass a thatched cottage on your left, continue ahead on a wider track and then onto a road. When you emerge from the trees with open hillside ahead, turn sharp right through a gate signed 'Castle Drogo and Fingle Bridge'. Follow this path uphill and round a sharp left-hand bend to continue on a path high above the Teign Valley with great views.

3 After a section of open hillside there is a small wooded cleft. Follow the path up some steps. At the road turn left and then bear right to reach the Castle Drogo visitor centre. Retrace your steps back to the path. Continue on the Hunter's Path towards Fingle Bridge. The path descends through oak woods. When you reach the road turn sharp right.

4 Cross the road from The Fingle Bridge Inn and follow the path upstream with the river on your left. After about 1 km you reach point 2. Retrace your steps to the start.

Castle Drogo, designed by Lutyens, is a fake castle built of granite.

further information

Castle Drogo is not a real castle. It is a country house designed by Lutyens in around 1910 for the Drewe family (whose wealth came from the Home & Colonial Stores). It is now owned by the National Trust.

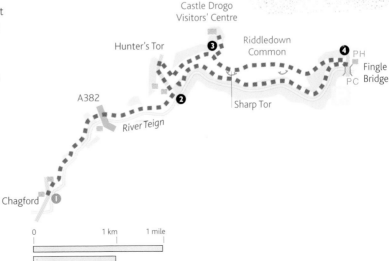

▲ Map: Explorer 116

▲ Distance: 10 km/6¼ miles

▲ Walk ID: 997 Al Rodger

Difficulty rating

Time

▲ Pub, Church, Wildlife, Birds, Great Views, Butterflies, Woodland

Symondsbury from North Chideock

Yeovil

A303

A3066

Axminster

Lyme Regis

Bridport

Dorch

A35

This is a circular walk through countryside west of Bridport, starting from the village of Chideock, home of the Chideock Martyrs. The route illustrates the charm of West Dorset at its best, and there are wonderful views to enjoy.

❶ Take the track with a cul-de-sac sign beside the cottage. Proceed uphill in a field with a fence on the left. Descend straight down the second field.

❷ Turn right up the hedged track. At the top of the hill continue down the Symondsbury track. Take the road to the left at the school.

❸ Beyond Symondsbury, turn right onto a track. Cross into a field on the left and make for the far-left corner. Cross the bridge and turn right, following the edge of the field to a gate. Cross the track into the field opposite. Cross the field half-left up to the corner of the hedge. Continue with the hedge on your right. At the hole through the hedge, take the path through the trees. Turn right at the junction. On the brow of the hill, turn left for rewarding views.

❹ Continue clockwise round the edge of the hilltop. Take the left path at the first junction. Continue down the steps towards the road and turn left. Turn right up the path between the housing and the hospital. Cross to the right-hand field. Keep ahead to cross back to the left-hand field at the gateway. Continue with the hedge on your right-hand side for two fields.

further information

John Cornelius, the Catholic chaplain of Lady Arundell, was arrested when visiting Chideock in 1594, along with two servants from Chideock and another visitor. The four were found guilty of treason. Refusing to embrace Protestantism, they were executed three months after their arrest.

A cross on the site of Chideock Castle commemorates these martyrs, and two others, Thomas Pilchard and Hugh Green.

The chiselled headlands around Lyme Regis create quite a distinctive coastline that is a fascinating place to explore.

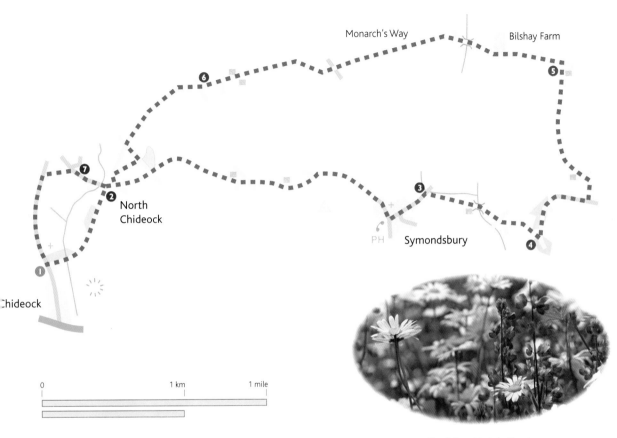

North
Chideock

Chideock

Monarch's Way

Bilshay Farm

Symondsbury

PH

0   1 km   1 mile

*Don't forget to take time to
stop on your walk and 'smell
the flowers'.*

❺ At the cottage turn left and follow the hedge. Cross the field to the right-hand of two gates into the next field. Head left towards the electricity pylon. Go over the stile into a garden, following the fence. Descend the field to a gate at the end of a line of posts. Cross the bridge and keep to the right side of the field. Go through the gap in the hedge into the next field. Follow the track up the left side to continue on the Monarch's Way.

❻ Go through both gates. Continue down the field and round the thicket on the sheep path. Follow the path and continue down the field towards the hedge, keeping the hedge on the right. Cross the bottom field to the left to reach a stile by a gate. Turn right to follow a track becoming a tarmac lane.

❼ Just before the junction, turn up the path on the left. Cross the field to a stile leading down to a path. Turn left at the road and continue back to the start.

access information

Turn north off the A35 in Chideock, west of Bridport, by the church on the road signed North Chideock. Just past the lane with the lodge on the corner, park on the side of the road with a slight verge.

A good bus service runs between Bridport and Lyme Regis and stops in Chideock, not far from the start.

▲ Map: Explorer OL 15

▲ Distance: 10 km/6¼ miles

▲ Walk ID: 572 Alan Kingsland

Difficulty rating

Time

▲ Hills or Fells, River, Pub, Church, National Trust, Wildlife, Birds, Flowers, Great Views

Hardy's Chess Piece Monument from Martinstown

This walk starts and finishes at St Martin's Church in the village of Martinstown, Dorset. The walk takes you through some fields and a copse to Great Hill. The walk then follows the ridge to the 'Chess Piece' that is Hardy's Monument.

❶ Cross the road from the church, then the footbridge to continue on a road. Once past the buildings the road bends first left then right. On the right bend join a footpath to the left. From the footpath sign the path leads across the field ahead. On the far side of this field go through a second to reach a young copse. Follow the path to the bottom of the valley. Then keep right as you travel up the valley to a farm track. Turn left, following the track to a field at the bottom of Great Hill.

❷ Take the chalky track up the first slope of Great Hill and into a field. Cross the middle of the field and go through the gate at the end. Continue across the next field to a hedge and signpost. Down to your left are views of Weymouth and Portland. Turn right and follow the path along the field edge and under the power lines. Take the path ahead at the rusty tanks. Go through a gate, up the hill between the gorse bushes to a second gate. Turn right and go through the gate, following the ridge path to the Chess Piece. At the road turn left and follow it up to the car park and monument.

❸ Retrace your steps back to the inland coastal path. Keep on the path to the junction.

❹ Turn left and follow the path to the farm buildings and road. At the road go through the gate and turn left. Follow this road to Pen Barn Farm.

❺ At the farm follow the path to the right, passing in front of the dark barn. Climb to the hilltop. Go through the gate and follow the field edge path down the slope to the next gate and track.

❻ Turn left onto the track, leaving to the right after a very short distance. Follow the footpath back down the valley to the copse you passed earlier. Retrace your steps to St Martin's Church.

access information

From the A35 roundabout west of Dorchester, follow signposts to Martinstown. Turn right into the village and head for St Martin's Church (500 m on the right).

Located on the highest point of the Blackdown area, the 21-metre Hardy's Monument is a landmark for any walker. Its site provides excellent views of the Dorset coast.

This footpath will lead you through some classic Dorset countryside, taking in picturesque villages and farms.

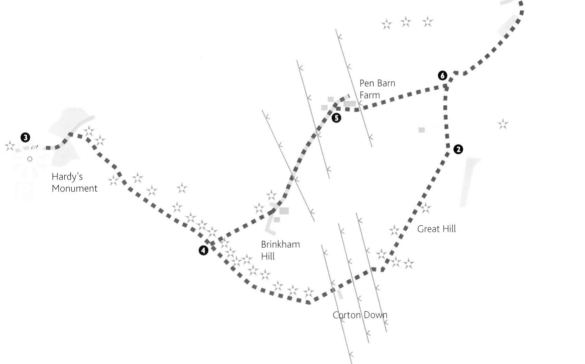

Martinstown

Pen Barn Farm

Hardy's Monument

Brinkham Hill

Great Hill

Corton Down

0   1 km   1 mile

further information

Hardy's Monument was built in 1848 to celebrate the life of Dorset's most famous maritime hero, Sir Thomas Masterman Hardy (of 'Kiss me, Hardy' fame). The monument is owned by the National Trust and is staffed from April to September. The climb to the parapet costs £1.

▲ Map: Explorer 141
▲ Distance: 5 km/3 miles
▲ Walk ID: 1081 Tony Brotherton

Difficulty rating

Time

Hills or Fells, Pub, Toilets, Museum, National Trust, Wildlife, Birds, Flowers, Great Views, Butterflies, Food Shop, Tea Shop

Around Glastonbury

A short tour of the town, including optional visits to the Abbey Ruins and Glastonbury Thorn, the Chalice Well and other points of religious interest, plus the obligatory pilgrimage to the Tor.

1 From the car park in Magdalene Street turn right, passing the entrance to the Abbey. Turn right onto the High Street. Walk up the High Street, passing the tourist information office on the left (the Lake Village Museum is housed here). Continue past St John's Church. Turn right along Lambrook Street, and carry on as far as the gateway of Abbey House on the right.

2 Turn up Dod Lane and take the driveway on the right, signed 'Footpath to Tor', to reach a squeeze stile. Follow the path uphill through fields to a lane and continue ahead.

3 Turn left to follow Bulwarks Lane to its end. At the road (Wick Hollow), turn uphill to reach the crossroads.

4 Take the lane to the right, with the Tor visible ahead, to reach a junction. Turn left and continue as far as the footpath to the Tor. Follow the path into a field, soon to climb to a stepped path. The path rises steeply to reach the summit and monument, where there are superb views.

5 Descend the Tor to reach a metal gate. Take the footpath downhill to Well House Lane. Turn left, then right at the road to arrive at Chalice Well. Turn right along Chilkwell Street to reach, on the left at the junction with Bere Lane, Somerset Rural Life Museum.

6 Turn left onto Bere Lane, then right downhill at the crossroads to return to Magdalene Street, to visit Alsmhouses Chapel. Turn left and continue past the former pumphouse to return to the start of the walk.

further information

Glastonbury was the first Christian sanctuary in Britain and is the legendary burial-place of King Arthur. The abbey ruins are open every day (except Christmas Day) from 9.30 a.m. to 6 p.m. (or dusk if earlier). Chalice Well is open every day – visiting times vary according to the season, so check beforehand if you wish to visit. The waters of the well were once considered curative. The Somerset Rural Life Museum is open 10 a.m. to 5 p.m., Tuesday to Friday, April to October, and at weekends from 2 to 6 p.m.

The distinctive and extraordinary mount of Glastonbury Tor can be seen from huge distances.

access information

Glastonbury is on the A361. Park in Magdalene Street, adjacent to Glastonbury Abbey grounds.

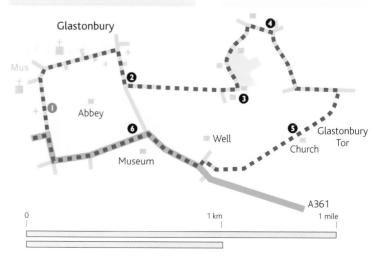

▲ Map: Explorer OL 45
▲ Distance: 5 km/3 miles
▲ Walk ID: 108 John Stewart

Difficulty rating

Time

▲ Hills or Fells, Great Views, Wildlife, Birds, Flowers

Beckbury Monument from Stanway

This circular walk in the heart of the Cotswolds involves a gentle climb up the escarpment to a point with a superb view. The return follows a section of The Cotswolds Way.

❶ From the Stanway crossroads, take the minor road heading right to Wood Stanway. Continue on this road and take the left fork. Turn right onto the lane at the start of Wood Stanway, then turn right beyond the cottage on the right.

❷ Go through the gate and turn sharp left. Head over the meadow towards the wood. Follow the grassy track uphill, keeping the wood on the right. Where the wood ends, cross the stile and turn sharp left, continuing towards the top of a steep bank.

❸ On top of the bank is a monument and viewpoint. Just to the back of the monument go through the wooden gate towards Beckbury Camp and continue on the grassy track, with the edge of the escarpment on the left. The path soon turns sharp right following the field boundary, terminating at a stony lane. Turn left and follow the track.

❹ At the road, turn left through the wooden gate onto a grassy path. The path descends the escarpment towards Wood Stanway. After a metal gate turn right and continue downhill, keeping the wall on your right. Follow the yellow markers over several stiles. Continue as the path meanders towards the village. At the valley bottom go through the metal gate onto the stony track. Pass the farm buildings and cottages.

❺ After the cottages turn right at the metal gate. Follow the path, keeping the field boundaries on the left until reaching a road. Turn left and continue to the start of walk.

access information

The walk starts at the Stanway crossroads on the B4077 road north west from Stow-on-the-Wold. There is good but limited off-road parking just south of the crossroads on the minor road leading to Wood Stanway.

Sheep graze in verdant, rolling countryside, in the Cotswolds near Stow-on-the-Wold.

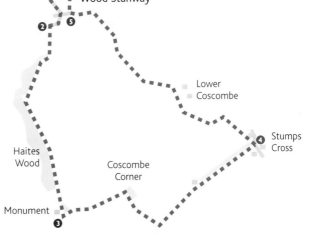

▲ Map: Explorer OL 14
▲ Distance: 5 km/3 miles
▲ Walk ID: 1426 Pat Roberts

Difficulty rating

Time

Wildlife, Birds, Flowers, Great Views, Butterflies, Mostly Flat, Woodland

Poors Allotment and the Jubilee Stone from Tidenham Chase

This easy, fairly level walk rewards you with fine views over the Severn Estuary to the Cotswolds to visit the Jubilee Stone.

1 Leave the car park and turn left onto the road. After 120 m, at the footpath sign, go right and continue through a series of gates to reach a minor road. Turn right.

2 Where the road swings sharply right, take the gate next to the footpath signs and follow the sign on the left. Head diagonally left, towards a stile in a fence. Cross the stile onto Poors Allotment, taking in the views over the Severn Estuary to the left.

3 Cross a small stream. Just before the large holly tree, the main path swings to the right. Ignore this path and head left, then turn left into the wood. Emerge from the wood into open ground and swing sharp right to reach a yellow marker post and then cross a stile onto a road. Turn left. After about 150 m, head right, past a barrier and into heathland, small trees and gorse. As the Gloucester Way comes in from the left, continue with it on the path furthest on the left.

4 At the Jubilee Stone, turn right and continue, ignoring any minor paths until you reach a clearing. At the clearing, ignore the track that comes in from the left and take the narrow path that goes off to the right. Follow this path through the wood. Ignore paths off to the left and the main road. When you reach a minor road, turn left.

5 Just before the main road take the stone stile on the right onto Poors Allotment. Stay on this grass track as it moves away from the trees and road on your left.

6 At the junction of paths, take the left fork, heading towards the trees and into the wood. Emerge from the wood through a metal kissing gate at the roadside opposite the car park.

access information

Parking is in an area adjoining the B4228, north east of Chepstow. There is a roadside sign to Offa's Dyke.

A view of the Severn Bridge, built across the Severn Estuary to provide a link between Wales and England, can be enjoyed during this walk.

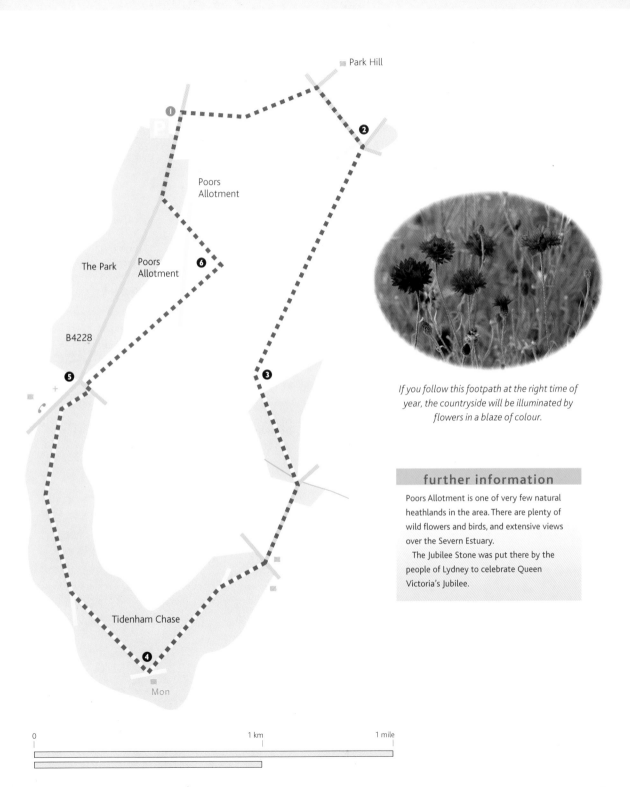

Park Hill

Poors
Allotment

The Park   Poors
Allotment

B4228

Tidenham Chase

Mon

*If you follow this footpath at the right time of
year, the countryside will be illuminated by
flowers in a blaze of colour.*

further information

Poors Allotment is one of very few natural
heathlands in the area. There are plenty of
wild flowers and birds, and extensive views
over the Severn Estuary.

The Jubilee Stone was put there by the
people of Lydney to celebrate Queen
Victoria's Jubilee.

0   1 km   1 mile

Index

acknowledgements

The publishers wish to thank the
following for the use of pictures:
COLLECTIONS: p. 22 Angela
Hampton
CORBIS: pps. 16 Wildcountry, 17
Michael Busselle, 18 Robert Estall, 24
Roy Westlake, 26 Jason Hawkes, 27
Bob Krist, 28/9 Michael Boys, 32 Bob
Krist, 33 Adam Woolfitt, 34 Michael
Busselle, 35 John Farmer, 40/1
Chinch Gryniewicz, 42 Peter Hulme,
44/5 Andrew Brown/Ecoscene, 46
Derek Coucher, 52 Bob Krist, 56
Michael Busselle, 58 Robert Estall,
61 Bob Krist, 62 David Dixon/Papillio
PAUL EDNEY: p. 53
GETTYIMAGES: pps. 30 Michael
Busselle/Stone, 50 Chris
Simpson/Stone
HUTCHISON PICTURE LIBRARY:
pps. 48 Robert Francis, 60
ALAN KINGSLAND: p. 59
PAT ROBERTS: pps. 15, 19, 41, 45,
47, 63
NICHOLAS RUDD JONES: pps. 12,
13
PETER SALENIEKS: pps.14, 36, 37, 49
JOHN THORN: pps. 8, 9, 10, 11, 20,
21, 38, 39, 43